Between The Crossroads
A Centennial History of Maurice, Louisiana

i

Front Cover

This church once stood as a symbol of community from 1918 to 1967. It was the third of four church buildings constructed for St. Alphonsus Church Parish in Maurice. The structure was razed in 1967 to make room for the present church building which was finished in 1968.

Between
The
Crossroads
A Centennial History of Maurice, Louisiana

By
Douglas L. Villien, Sr.

Villien Publishing
Baton Rouge 2012

This book is printed on acid-free paper and meets the guidelines certified by the FSC-U.S.
Graphics and consulting for this book is provided by Randy Bringhurst.

First Printing, July 2012

ISBN-10: 0985816910
ISBN-13: 978-0-9858169-1-9
(black and white)

To

Polo & Tookoo

And

Karen, the love of my life

Contents

Acknowledgements

Information and materials gathered for this work was based on years of research, collections of photographs, family history notes, newspapers and historical books. Many people throughout South Louisiana were extremely helpful to my research and compiling of this work. Acknowledgement must first go to generations of those families and authors that recognized the value of protecting their relics and keepsakes over time.

I am grateful to the unknown and unrecognized individuals who preserved photographs and notes that contained history about Maurice. And to the residents of the area and in the Village of Maurice who preserved bits and pieces of their history for future generations. And I owe special gratitude to those who were interviewed for this book. Their information filled the gaps of my own memories which go back to my youth.

I am heavily indebted to and offer thanks to my cousin, Berta Villien Winch, who shared an extraordinary amount of her time in interviews. Her personal dedication in recounting of many episodes and events in Maurice is unsurpassed. Beyond expectations, she provided technical assistance on a plethora of subjects throughout this work. And, thanks to her teaching and writing skills, she provided qualified review of grammar and composition.

The following, are due special thanks; to educators for opening the doors of their schools: Wendy Stoute, former Principal of Cecil Picard Elementary Maurice School; Greg Theriot, Principal of North Vermilion High School, Ivy Landry, former Assistant Principal of North Vermilion High School; and to Elizabeth Landry, Edgar Baudoin, Jr., and Elgin Prejean Baudoin for the courtesy and access to their private collections.

I express my appreciation to Fr. O. Joseph Breaux, Pastor, St. Alphonsus Catholic Church and Mary Beth Dupuis for providing access to archives and church records. And to both church parishes in Maurice for providing an abundance of information greater than this work could absorb.

To Dr. Paul Villien, Sr., historian, preservationist and philanthropist for his life time of genealogy research and collection of historical facts about this community and its families. Great appreciation is owed to his unraveling centuries of his own family history, documenting and preserving much detail that would have otherwise been lost by the generation of today. Thanks to his unselfish and keen foresight in preserving artifacts in memoriam for future generations.

For their time and assistance I am grateful to the Maurice Volunteer Fire Department, especially Matthew Trahan and Carroll Comeaux.

I am in great appreciation to Loubert Trahan, Doris and Wallace Broussard, Dr. David G. Trahan, Garrett Broussard, Johnette Broussard, Francine Broussard Mathiew, Tasha Villien Leger, Gerald Dartez, David O. Trahan, Sonia LeBlanc Comboy and Jackie LeBlanc Truitt for their indulgence of time and contributions from their family collections. And to my friends on the Face Book page, *If you grew up in Maurice...then you remember*, your information is invaluable to the community.

This book could not have been possible without the extraordinary assistance provided by employees of the Village of Maurice. Honorable mention goes to Judy C. Broussard, Joan D. Methvin, former Mayor Bob Ferguson and Mayor Wayne Theriot.

Special thanks to Brock Bravo for his invaluable recommendations on editing of grammar, composition and book format.

I am immensely appreciative and owe gratitude to my brother, Dr. O. Paul Villien, Jr., for his documentation of our foreign and domestic family heritage. His books on the *Villien-Chaty Family, Volume 1 and 2* were invaluable resources. The volumes transcend hundreds of years of family history and brought us to the period that casts first light on key subjects in this work.

I am thankful for my loving children Heather Villien Frantz, Holly Villien Brown and Douglas Villien, Jr. for their encouragement during the course of this writing; and my sweet wife, Karen, for her understanding, patience and faithful support to its end.

Preface

I've always felt as though I was a native of two towns, Abbeville and Maurice. Like so many others throughout the south, we lived in one town and grandparents lived in another. Part of my life growing up was all about Maurice and the homestead of my ancestors. Much of my childhood was spent on the family farm and streets of Maurice with cousins and friends. Children from our generation were taught to appreciate our culture, heritage, folklore and the value of tradition. That seed inspired a level of interest for me to know more about my ancestry.

When I first started this project, I wanted to write a biography about my great-grandfather, Jean-Maurice Villien (Maurice Villien), founder of the Village of Maurice. The biography was intended to be much more detailed than previous writings. However, in delving into his background, I discovered that his impact was much greater than I once believed. I learned his original intention was simply to set out from his homeland as an energetic young entrepreneur and come to America for new opportunities. Events after arrival here perhaps changed all of that. His neutrality as a French citizen meant little to the wanton and greed of Union Troops during the Civil War.

I was fascinated about his trek through those beginnings in the Teche Valley to his final destination in Vermilion Parish. Lack of available information made my endeavor seem like it may succeed only to a level that had been previously written. From my research, I was able to shed new light on previous writings about his life. His own successes in business availed him an opportunity to market a plan to build a "small city" on the coastal prairie of north Vermilion Parish.

I found that he was not alone in his endeavor. His biography and that of others were part of a greater story that should be documented and dovetailed into one writing. I could not separate his biography from the beginnings of this community. I discovered that I needed to tell the story about the village. In the beginning, it was a place known as Mauriceville, then Maurice, and finally, the Village of Maurice in 1911. Though vignettes had been written before, none have been entirely comprehensive about its history. I felt that this project fell into a category called "somebody ought to do it". I've enjoyed the challenge of being that "somebody". Little did I realize how much I would learn through telling a century-old story.

I learned more fully about how the community came to be at its present location and that most everything happened *between the crossroads* in Maurice.

I Jared Young Sanders, Governor of the State of Louisiana…
Do hereby issue this, my proclamation, declaring the said
Village a corporation in law…
December 27, 1911

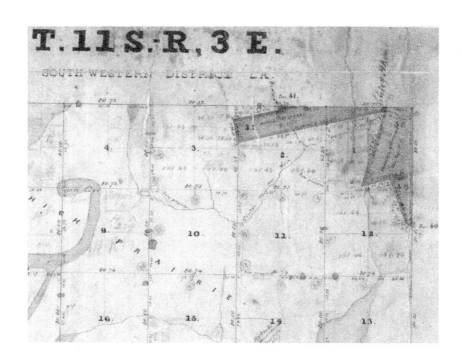

Composite Survey Map of Township Eleven South, Range Three East, South Western District, Vermilion Parish, Louisiana. Survey compiled by Michael McCarty, 1808; Evan Bowles, 1808; Maxfield Ludlow, 1809 – 1812; William Johnson, 1817 – 1821; John Boyd, 1841 – 1848; and John Campbell, 1843 – 1852.

Between The Crossroads

Early Years

Fig. 1.1 *At the home of Dr. J.A. Villien, his horse and buggy were kept in a buggy shed in the back of the house. When Dr. Villien needed to make a house-call, he would send word to Joe Tani, the farmhand, and in a short time the horse and buggy was ready to go.*

Early Years

1

Land Divisions

A people of pride and politeness, Cajuns find much of their family history in what was known as the County of the Attakapas, originally both a civil and military county established during Spanish and French occupancy and one of Louisiana's early political divisions. The district was named for the Attakapas Indians. Spanish, Acadians and French came to settle in the region and soon following the Louisiana Purchase, the district became subject to further divisions called parishes. The parishes of St. Martin, St. Mary, Lafayette, Iberia and in 1844, the Parish of Vermilion were formed from the division.

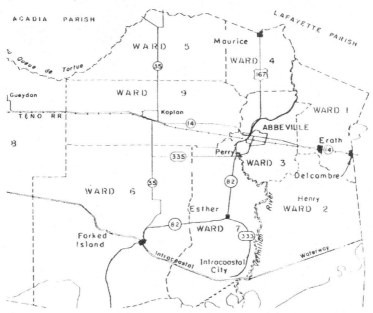

Fig. 1.2 *Ward Map of north Vermilion Parish*

Vermilion Parish was further divided into nine wards. Ward Four was commonly known as Broussard Cove and consisted of an area from north of Meaux to the Lafayette Parish boundary and eastward to the Vermilion Bayou. The Village of Maurice was shaped from large sections of land in Ward Four. The terrain in this ward consisted of open prairie, tall grasses and many small ponds, natural depressions, known as *des trous de toreau*. The land was particularly attractive to settlers for its nearly year-round growing season and for grazing cattle. Timber land of venerable oaks and cypress were principally along the bountiful waterways of Bayou Vermilion or Coulee Ile des Cannes.

3

Origin of the Founder

Much has been written about the Acadians who settled this area, but not generally known, are those foreign French who nested amongst them. One such forebear in the last wave of immigration gave cause for this writing.

For an understanding of how the Village of Maurice began and its early years, one should know the origin of its founder and his journey here. Brothers, Jean-Maurice and Joseph-Etienne Villien hoped to seek out new opportunities in America and settle in an area that reminded them of their homeland. Maurice and Etienne were from the hamlet of Vulmix in the commune of Bourg St-Maurice, the largest French-speaking town in the Tarentaise Valley within the heart of the French Alps. Bourg St-Maurice was described as a peaceful little

Fig. 1.3 Brothers Joseph-Etienne and Jean-Maurice Villien posed for a final photograph in 1855 before departing for America

market town located in a large basin at the foot of Mt. Blanc. They were descendants of dairy farmers who were known for a variety of cheeses.

Maurice and Etienne arrived in New Orleans in 1855. Etienne accidentally drowned in the Mississippi River shortly after arriving in New Orleans.

When Maurice departed his homeland, he was a subject of Charles Albert, King of Sardinia (he was a Sardinian). The status of his citizenship changed while in the United States. He became a naturalized French subject of Napoléon III by French referendum annexing La Savoie to France in 1860. For Maurice, the status of being a naturalized citizen of France would become an important legal issue later in his life.

Following Etienne's death Maurice moved west to the French-speaking area along Bayou Teche between Jeanerette and New Iberia. There he established a mercantile business at Île Piquant, today Patoutville, in then St. Mary Parish. His general store was known as *Le Petit Magasin*.

Like other foreign-French, Maurice was politically inactive and indifferent to the North and South discord of the 1860s. He had no interest in becoming involved with Southern rights or slaves. He was an energetic young businessman engaged in marketing wares throughout the region. He thought he was protected as a citizen of France and immune to engagement with army troops. He disagreed with the encroachment of the Civil War into his daily life. However, without regard for Maurice's neutrality as a French citizen,

Union Army General Michael K. Lawler and his troops twice plundered Maurice's store on October 15 and 16, 1863. He was victim of the army's wanton and greed.

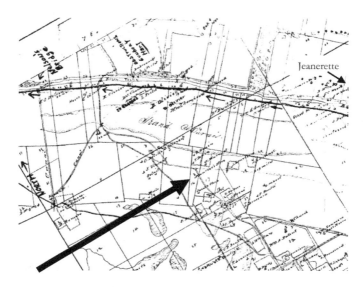

Fig. 1.4 *This 1863 Plat Map depicts part of St. Mary Parish near Bayou Teche. Shown here, is the site of Maurice Villien's Store at Île Piquant (Patoutville) between New Iberia and Jeanerette. The site is bordered on the east by present day College Road near Enterprise Plantation. Jean-Maurice resided here from April 13, 1861 to August 20, 1866.*

After the Civil War, Maurice left Île Piquant to establish another store on a site along the busy waterway of Bayou Vermilion. Here, ca. 1867, he met his bride to be, Marie-Marguerite Chaty, a native of the Youngsville-Milton area.

On the west bank of Bayou Vermilion at a location called Milton Crossing, Maurice established a new store or depot. From Milton, he would sell his wares by horse drawn hack throughout the countryside in Vermilion, St. Mary and Lafayette parish.

Homesteading in Vermilion Parish
Sections of public land in Ward Four were still available and for sale to the general public between 1860 and 1890. Around the end of 1868, Maurice and Marie settled on a tract three miles west of Milton and built a store and home along a wagon road that traversed east-west across the land. In 1873 they filed application for a land grant on the northeast quarter of Section 11 (T11S, R3E). Their patent for homestead was certified in 1878. They had become pioneers of commerce to an area of lush vegetation on high land of *Prairie Vermilion*. The homestead was near the center of their tract in a small wooded area, an island of trees, on a sea of grassland.

5

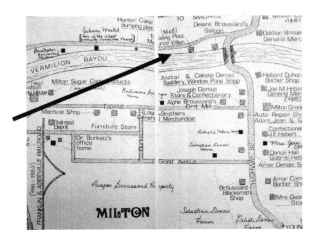

Fig. 1.5 *Map of Milton. After the Civil War Maurice married Marie Chaty and settled in Vermilion Parish on the west bank of Bayou Vermilion. Between 1867 and 1868, Maurice's Trading Post was located at the ferry landing known as Milton Crossing.*

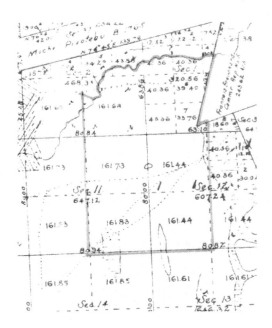

Fig. 1.6 *A Homestead Map of 1881 showing Quarter Sections and an outline of the original Maurice corporate limits. Wagon roads and trails meandered aimlessly across the prairie.*

6

Fig. 1.7 *An aerial photo of The Grove on Prairie Vermilion in 1970. This view, looking southeast, is where Jean-Maurice and Marie Villien established a home and a store known as Le Magasin à Maurice. The store faced the east (left) and was located on the south side of the pond.*

The small stand of trees and pond was located near the center of their tract. Their home stood on the opposite side of the pond from the store which was called *le Magasin à Maurice*. Family and neighbors referred to the location of the site as "The Grove". While living there, Maurice and Marie had five children, Joseph Angelle (b. 1870) and Jean Maurice, Jr. (b.1875) lived to adulthood. Maurice and Marie would frequently host a Catholic mass in their home when a priest from Abbeville would make a periodic visit.

Fig. 1.8 *An artist's rendering of Jean-Maurice Villien home site in The Grove.*

Fig. 1.9 *Jean-Maurice Villien*
(1831 – 1902)

Fig. 1.10 *Marie Chaty Villien*
(1847 – 1932)

Planning to Build a City
The small store attracted settlers to form a community and by 1875 when Jean-Maurice became a naturalized American citizen, the sparsely populated area had become known as Mauriceville with a population of less than fifty people. Broussard Cove population had grown to approximately thirteen hundred.

Maurice Villien envisioned bringing folks together and forming a community. He planned a grid of streets and lots. He sought to attract businesses and residents to the community and understood that stores, churches and schools were necessary for success. His vision was to build a "small city", similar to his birthplace in France. Maurice understood the importance of creating lots on both sides of a primary road. The success of his plan relied on a partnership with an adjacent land owner of Section 12.

A Partnership
Maurice Villien joined into partnership with Corine Broussard. Together they implemented a subdivision plan and sold lots for commercial and residential use. On January 3, 1885, the partners announced their forthcoming sale in the *Abbeville Meridional*: "Notice: A certain number of lots in the town of Mauriceville, will be sold to the highest bidders, on Saturday July 22, at 1 p.m., M. Villien, Corine Broussard, Proprietors".

Old meandering trails and roads once crossed the prairie aimlessly. Many land owners, like Mr. Villien and Mrs. Broussard, relocated the roads to the section

8

boundaries as they fenced-in their properties. Landowners usually maintained the roads along their boundaries as they maintained their fencerows. The road along the boundary between Sections 11 and 12 became a straight north-south route as it followed other section boundaries leading from Maurice to Abbeville. Throughout the area other section roads were formed in an east-west direction to create a grid pattern. The section roads became primary routes of travel. When Maurice Villien laid out plans for a city, his plan followed the boundaries between Sections 1, 2, 11 and 12. The two roads came to be named Maurice Avenue (North-South) and Lafayette Street (East-West). About the same time, another east-west road was formed southward at the next intersection of section boundaries, Etienne Road, named after Etienne Broussard. By 1886 Mr. Villien had erected the first structure of Mauriceville on a tract of land bordering Maurice Avenue. The building was a Catholic Church which he planned to donate to the Bishop of New Orleans. The site was located along the west side of Maurice Avenue *between the crossroads* of Lafayette Street and Etienne Road.

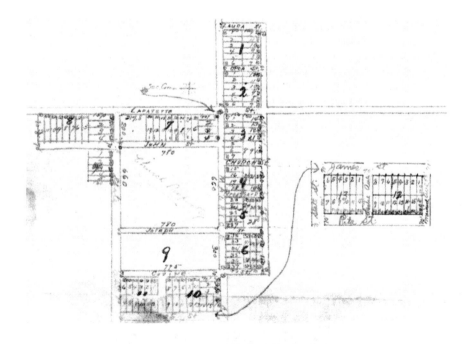

Fig. 1.11 *First Plan of Maurice*

Corine Broussard was of seventh generation Acadian descent from Jean Francois Broussard. She was the daughter of Camille Jean Francois Broussard (descendant of Jean Francois Baptiste Broussard and Hortense Broussard of St. Martinville) and Aurelia Amelia [sic] Broussard (daughter of Edouard Broussard and Euphemie Sylvanie Broussard). Corine Marie and three siblings Maria, Jean Treville and Albert Camille each inherited significant acreage in Section 12 (*the southeast quadrant of Maurice*) from Camille J.F. Broussard. Camille J.F. homesteaded the southwest quarter of Section 12 in 1860 and later acquired practically the whole of Section 12, including homesteads of Joseph Hernandez and John Smith. Corine Broussard married Hilaire Broussard

Fig. 1.12 Corine M. Broussard was a prominent businesswoman, benefactor and founding developer of Maurice. (1867 – 1945)

and later built a prominent home and small store located in the northwest quadrant of Section 12 on the northeast corner of Maurice Avenue and Church Street.

Fig. 1.13 La Chapelle à Maurice, built in 1886 (Église de St. Alphonse à Mauriceville) is the second oldest Catholic Church in Vermilion Parish.

10

Building a Chapel

Maurice Villien wanted to bring a permanent pastor to the area and began negotiations with the Archbishop of New Orleans. By 1886 he built a church on a large parcel of land in the northeast corner of his homestead. The church acquired the name, "La Chapelle à Maurice". It was among the first of the buildings constructed on the grid-work of streets. In 1889 Archbishop Perché accepted the donation of ten acres of land, a rectory and church building and assigned a pastor. The name of the church was accepted as "Église de St. Alphonse à Mauriceville." Father Alphonse LeQuilleuc was the first pastor. St. Alphonsus Catholic Church became the second oldest Catholic Church in Vermilion Parish. In effect, "La Chapelle à Maurice" became the cornerstone and foundation of the village as businesses and people were attracted to build near the church.

First Families

When Maurice and Marie Villien came to settle here in 1868, they were not the first in this corner of Vermilion Parish. In the area known as Broussard Cove and along Bayou Vermilion large sections of land were already settled. Sections one, two, eleven and twelve, of Township 11 South, Range 3 East (T11S, R3E), were homesteaded lands of what eventually became the new settlement of Maurice. Portions of these sections were homesteaded generally between 1860 and 1898 and later incorporated in 1911. Many of the *first families* that homesteaded were Granger, Ruffin, Vincent, Arceneaux, Banquerel, Villien, Pelletier, Hernandez, Smith and Broussard. Some of these families continue to own portions of their homesteads to this day.

Section 1
    Jean Granger, 1873
    Pemberton Ruffin, 1880
    Valsin Vincent, 1883
    Aurelien Arceneaux, 1836
    Robert Banquerel, 1836
Section 2
    Jean Granger, 1898
Section 11
    (*Jean*) Maurice Villien, 1878
    Christine Pelletier, 1898
Section 12
    Joseph Hernandez, 1860
    John J. Smith, 1860
    Camille J.F. (*Jean Francois*) Broussard, 1860

However, names which are thought of as *early families* of Maurice are those which were noted in government, church and school records. The families of Bacque, Baudoin, Baumgardner, Broussard, Brumfield, Carmier [sic], Catalon, Chargois, Clark, Comeaux, Dartez, Dronet, Duhon, Fuselier, Hebert,

Lalande, Landry, LeBlanc, Leger, Montet, Mouton, Nugent, Picard, Richard, Trahan, Villien, and Vincent are repeatedly found in record books and archives of the community. Many other family names are in St. Alphonsus church records but were not residents of the community. The church parish of St. Alphonsus is geographically much larger than the incorporated area of Maurice.

Some of the settlers that filed application for Federal Land Grants on lands adjacent and outside the corporate limits of Maurice were:

Section 3
>Joseph Michel, 1891
>John Clark, Jr., 1888
>Dapalline Breaux, 1883
>Henry Johnson, 1882
>Louis Simon, Jr., 1879
>Athemas Meaux, 1873

Section 10
>Desiré O. Broussard, 1860
>V. Broussard, 1860
>Placide Duhon, 1860
>Thomas Coopwood, 1860

Section 11
>Arvillien Catalon, 1878
>Sevenne Meaux, 1886

Section 13
>Joseph Clark, 1881
>Jules Fuselier, 1891
>Marion Chargois, 1888

Section 14
>John Rykoski, 1860
>Lessine Trahan, 1860

First Business, Post Office and School

The first commercial establishment in Maurice was that of Jean-Maurice Villien. In 1894, Maurice moved his home and business from *The Grove* to Maurice Avenue, a road named after him and later became the main route between Lafayette and Abbeville (also designated La. Highway 43 and U.S. Highway167). His home was of such size that it was divided into three parts. Two sections were given to local residents while the rear section of the home was moved onto a lot on Maurice Avenue. This rear section of the home was converted to a mercantile and retained the name *Le Magasin à Maurice*. His son, Dr. Joseph A. Villien, soon after built a medical office adjacent to the store. It is believed that his medical office was the second business establishment in town.

Fig. 1.14 *An artist's rendering of Le Magasin à Maurice as it looked in circa 1895.*

Fig. 1.15 *Le Magasin à Maurice, 2009*

By September 1895 area population had grown and the need for improved mail service led to the establishment of a United States Post Office at Maurice's store. Maurice Villien became the first postmaster. It was then that the name of the community changed from Mauriceville to Maurice.

In July 1899 the first Maurice School was built on a one acre site donated by Maurice Villien. The site was located between Lafayette Street (Indian Bayou Road) and John Street. On this site were two wood framed buildings which faced St. Alphonsus Church. The smaller of the two buildings was designated as the primary school and the second building was for the junior high school.

Jean-Maurice Villien died in 1902. Mrs. Villien, "Mémère", continued to run the store with her two sons, Dr. Joseph A. Villien and Jean-Maurice Villien, Jr., until 1916 when she relinquished her share of ownership to them. Mémère lived adjacent to her son's medical office on Maurice Avenue. Circa 1916 a new store was constructed at the corner of Maurice Avenue and Church Street. The old store was moved further back on its lot and became a warehouse behind the new building. After completion of the new store, the name was changed from *Le Magasin à Maurice* to *Villien Brothers and Company*, Joseph and Jean Villien, proprietors.

Fig. 1.16 Dr. Joseph A. Villien

Fig. 1.17 Jean M. Villien, Jr.
"T-N'oncle"

The original store remained a warehouse until 2009 when the Bank of Abbeville purchased the site. In 2010 the Bank of Abbeville donated the old building to the Maurice Historical Preservation Society and the society renamed it, *Le Musée à Maurice*. The building was moved to its present site on Chief H. Fred Avenue. The land was donated by Dr. Marc J. Villien to the Maurice Historical Preservation Society. The building has traveled nearly

Fig. 1.18 Villien Brothers and Company, built ca. 1916, Dr. Joseph A., Jean M. and Mrs. Jean-Maurice Villien, proprietors.

full circle as the land it now sits on is part of the original Jean-Maurice Villien homestead and only several hundred yards from *The Grove*.

Fig. 1.19 Villien Brothers store shown with the original Le Magasin à Maurice structure shown behind Villien Brothers.

Fig. 1.20 Villien Brothers closed for business in 1968. In 1969 Raymond Broussard, owner of Ray's Appliances, occupied the building until 1992 followed by the Maurice Flea Market. The Flea Market occupied the building until 2009 after the Villien family sold the site to the Bank of Abbeville and Trust.

15

Early Acadian Landowners

Before Maurice Villien arrived here, the *first homesteads* were established by settlers such as Jean Granger, Joseph Hernandez, John J. Smith and Camille Jean Francois Broussard. Additional Land Grants followed and included names as: Arvillien Catalon, Christine Pelletier, Sevenne Meaux, Pemberton Ruffin and Valsin Vincent.

Fig. 1.21
Camille Jean Francois Broussard

Fig. 1.22
Aurelia Amelia Broussard

Broussard descendants farmed the land long before Jean-Maurice Villien settled in Section 11. The Broussard families joined-in early development and were an integral part in founding the Village of Maurice. One of the most noted settlers of the time was Camille Jean Francois Broussard. Camille Jean Francois was the son of Jean Francois Baptiste Broussard and Hortense Broussard, and the grandson of Francois Broussard and Pelagie Landry. Camille Jean Francois grew up on his father's plantation located on Bayou Vermilion near present day Pinhook Bridge in Lafayette. His grandfather, Francois, was born in Nova Scotia and came to Louisiana with his father, commandant of the Acadians, Joseph dit Beau Soleil Broussard. Francois eventually settled on land purchased from an Attakapas Indian chief on Bayou Vermilion north of Milton.

Francois owned vast tracts of land that radiated east and west from the Vermilion Bayou. At Maurice, the western edge of his land extended to present day Andre Road. And the breadth of his land spanned from Coulee Île des Cannes to near Milton. Many current day Maurice and Milton residents descend from Francois Broussard. Camille Jean Francois married Aurelia Amelia Broussard, daughter of Edouard Theophile Broussard and Euphemie Belizaire Broussard.

Camille Jean Francois had nine children but only four survived to adulthood. His adult children were, Jean Treville, a well-known business man in Lafayette Parish, Marie (Maria), Albert Camille, a noted cattle rancher in Vermilion Parish and Corine Marie, a prominent businesswoman and benefactor in Maurice. All four married and raised families in the Maurice area. Camille Jean Francois homesteaded the southwest quarter of Section 12, T11S, R3E in 1860 and later acquired other parcels. His holdings consisted of the southeast quadrant of the Village of Maurice and his home was in the vicinity of East Lafayette Street. Broussard Street in Maurice is named in honor of Camille Jean Francois Broussard.

By the mid 1890s, a piece of Prairie Vermilion had taken shape in the form of a "small city". The northern crossroads of the village were located at the intersection of Maurice Avenue and Lafayette Street, formed by the borders of Sections 1, 2, 11 and 12; and the southern crossroads were located at the intersection of Maurice Avenue and Etienne Road formed by the borders of Sections 11, 12, 13 and 14. Between these crossroads, Jean-Maurice Villien fulfilled his dream and carved the first earthen roads into the land covered by a picturesque sea of tall grasses. In the beginning, he built a church, a school and a store. City blocks and lots were sold to newcomers and entrepreneurs. These were the early years of the village, when folks were moving to a place called Mauriceville and bringing with them, industriousness, individualism, adaptability and pride in their cultural history.

Fig. 1.23 *Gifts from Jacques-Marie Villien*
Jean-Maurice Villien, a progenitor in the "Early Years" of Mauriceville, was memorialized by a bronze bust (top photo) commissioned by Jacques-Marie Villien, brother of Jean-Maurice. Jacques-Marie lived in France and employed a French sculptor to make two bronze busts, one of his brother Jean-Maurice and one of himself (bottom left photo). The original busts are in possession of the Lastie Maurice Villien family. In 1990, Dr. Paul O. Villien, Jr., great-grandson of Jean-Maurice, commissioned artist Ken Herrin of New Orleans to make three duplicate sets of the bronze busts. The duplicate sets are in possession of Dr. Paul O. Villien, Jr., Dr. Richard P. Villien and Douglas L. Villien, Sr.

Jacques-Marie also commissioned a French artisan to make a unique hand-carved desk featuring wooden sculptures of Marie, wife of Jean-Maurice Villien, their two sons, Joseph A. and Jean M., their wives, Octavie Broussard and Ellen Suire, and the children of Joseph, Jacques Cyr and Rita. The desk is now in possession of Edward Villien, great-grandson of Jean-Maurice Villien.

Jacques-Marie Villien commissioned the original bronze busts and hand-carved desk as gifts to his nephew, Dr. Joseph A. Villien.

18

Beginnings of Business

Fig. 2.1 *The beginnings of commerce in Maurice relied on area farming. Farmers of the prairies learned to alternate between growing rice, cotton and grazing cattle. They were very efficient in the use of their land. (Photo of Tom and Esther Baudoin on Wilson Road; Placide Broussard house in background.)*

Beginnings of Business
2

Broussard's Store

The first fourteen blocks established by Maurice's plan encompassed the ten acre site of St. Alphonsus Catholic Church. The street grid of the village was a reality with an active church, school and the first mercantile at the center of the community. Soon to follow were other businesses along Maurice Avenue.

Fig. 2.2 Albert Benedict Broussard (1868-1908) managed the Broussard Store when it first opened around 1895. The store was constructed by Lafayette businessman Jean Treville Broussard. Jean "Tee" Camille Broussard and Adonis Picard purchased the store from Mrs. Jean Treville Broussard around 1917.

Fig. 2.3 Albert Camille Broussard (1858-1906) was a prominent cattle and horse rancher of the area. He was an early cowboy of Vermilion Parish and frequently drove cattle to market in Texas and New Orleans. He married, Marie Leocadie Nunez, daughter of Vermilion Parish Senator and Representative Joseph Adrien Nunez.

In September of 1894, Jean Treville Broussard, a prominent businessman of Lafayette and Vermilion Parish lived on a one hundred thirty acre tract in Maurice and announced that he was hauling five wagon loads of lumber from Lafayette to Mauriceville. He was going to build a large store in the new town and his son-in-law, Albert Benedict Broussard will manage the business according to an article in the *Lafayette Advertiser*. Albert B., at the time was married to Cecile Broussard (Albert Benedict was the son of Marcel G. Broussard and Coralie Caruthers). Jean Treville built an impressive two-story mercantile with attached living quarters. The building was constructed on the southeast corner of Maurice Avenue and Broussard Street. The second floor was also living quarters but later became part of the retail space.

Following Cecile's death in 1898, Albert Benedict married Aminthe Comeaux (daughter of Lauzin Comeaux and Azema Broussard) and continued to run the store until his death in 1908. Ownership of the store remained in the name of Jean Treville Broussard and then his widow, Matilde Breaux Broussard, until 1918. Jean "Tee" Camille Broussard, a native of Maurice, apprenticed and clerked at Maurice Villien's Store before he purchased the Broussard Store from Matilde. Tee-Camille was the son of Albert Camille Broussard and Marie Leocadie Nunez. Marie Leocadie was also of prominent Vermilion Parish family heritage. She was the daughter of a well known planter, rancher and former State Representative and Senator, Joseph Adrien Nunez of Abbeville and Olivia Guidry of St. Martin Parish.

Tee-Camille and his wife, Ada Hebert Broussard, then entered into business partnership with his sister Marie Leonie and brother-in-law, Adonis Picard to form the Broussard-Picard Store. The business continued in operation until circa 1938.

Tee-Camille and Ada had eleven children, Edward, Doris, Lastie, Claude, Wallace, Gladys, John, Alice, Willie, Walter and Faye Marie. Ada was the daughter of Lastie Hebert and Marie Fabre. Edward opened a lumber and paint store adjacent to the Broussard-Picard store. Business partner, Adonis Picard, was the son of Aristide Picard and Azema Broussard. Aristide and two brothers, Adolph and Augustin, were French immigrants. Aristide and Azema had twelve children and owned a business in Maurice.

Fig. 2.4 *Broussard – Picard General Merchandise Store*
Jean Camille "Tee-Camille" Broussard is shown standing at the far left of the porch and his horse "Beauty" at the hitching post on a snow-covered day.

21

Corine Broussard, business partner of Maurice Villien, married Hilaire [sic] Broussard in 1895. They too established a mercantile at the center of Maurice. The building was small compared to the Villien Brothers and the Broussard-Picard stores. Hilaire Broussard's store was located on the northeast corner of Maurice Avenue and Church Street. Many years after the store went out of business, the building was converted into a movie theater.

Fig. 2.5 Jean Camille and Ada Hebert Broussard, ca 1918

Fig. 2.6 Hilaire Broussard

Fig. 2.7 Home of Corine and Hilaire Broussard, built before 1900. The home is on the northwest corner of Maurice Avenue and Church Street. Three of their children, Ann, Camille (Teet), and Paul lived in the home after Corine and Hilaire died. Joseph Clyve Broussard, son of Louis Broussard, inherited the home from his aunt Ann and uncles "Teet" and Paul. The home was later passed on to Clyve's daughter and current occupant, Johnette Broussard.

Fig. 2.8 *The home of Dr. Joseph A. and Octavia Broussard Villien. This historic home was built in 1895, the year they were married. Octavia died in 1906, Dr. Villien re-married Annette Maude Gaidry in 1915. She resided in the home until 1992. The home is presently owned by Dr. Marc J. Villien, grandson of Dr. and Mrs. J.A. Villien. Today it is one of few Vermilion Parish structures on the National Register of Historic Places.*

Villien Estate

Dr. Joseph A. Villien, son of Jean-Maurice and Marie Chaty Villien, completed medical school in 1890. He practiced as an associate physician for a brief time in Milton and around 1894 established an office in Maurice. His first office here was built on Maurice Avenue. At the center of the block between Church Street and Broussard Street, from north to south, were his office, Le Magasin à Maurice and his parent's home. Both corners of the block remained vacant and were later occupied by Villien Brothers Store (Maurice Ave. and Church St.) and the Bank of Maurice (Maurice Ave. and Broussard). Following Maurice Villien's death in 1902, Dr. Villien, his brother, Jean, and his mother continued management of the store.

By the year he married, in 1895, Dr. Villien built a large Victorian style home on a portion of the homestead settled by his parents. He continued the business of planting and farming started by his father and eventually expanded the business by acquiring additional land. The farm operation became quite complex. The farm business, included raising beef cattle, produced rice, corn, sweet potatoes, cotton, and other crops.

Dr. Villien understood the importance of efficiently moving products from farm to market. His business interests and involvement on a railroad committee contributed to bringing railway service closer to Maurice. The Franklin & Abbeville Railroad was completed in 1910, from New Iberia to Milton. The rail line operated approximately twenty years until ca. 1930, when the state began to pave many roads.

Fig. 2.9 Medical office of Dr. Joseph A. Villien, Sr. Dr. Villien's second office was built ca. 1921. His first office was located on the north side of Le Magasin à Maurice on Maurice Avenue. In the early years it was not uncommon for the working class country folk to barter their farm products such as chickens, eggs or cochon de lait for medical treatment or city goods from the Villien or Broussard stores.

Farming

Farming played an important role in the local economy. Large scale farming of rice and cotton changed the tall grass prairies to a point where groves of trees appeared as islands on the horizon. Above the crops and fields, one could see a neighbor's farm house at far distances. Around the turn of the century almost every community growing cotton or rice had its own gin or mill. Farmers made record profits from either crop. Cotton crops of the area were large enough for Leroy and Maurice to each have a cotton gin and for Maurice to have two rice mills. Typical cotton and rice farm operations employed the whole family including the children who often worked in the fields after school. Some years, the beginning of the school term was delayed so students could help with harvesting and not miss school.

Fig. 2.10 Maurice Cotton Gin

Fig. 2.11 Trahan Rice Mill

Cotton production here diminished significantly between 1900 and 1920 after the cotton bowl weevil devastated the industry but later came back strong. Rice, sugar cane, corn, and sweet potatoes comprised the greatest percent of other agricultural crops during that time. Cotton once again increased in production between 1925 and 1960 but eventually yielded to rice production, which required less labor to produce.

The Maurice Cotton Gin was built in 1925 and the founding board members included local businessmen Cyprien D. Trahan, H. A. Bacque, Edmond Richard, Alexis LeBlanc, Dr. J.A. Villien, Jean-Camille Broussard and John M. Broussard. Soon to follow were corporations such as Julian LeBlanc's Rice Mill and the Trahan Rice Mill and Seed Company. By the late nineteen twenties Maurice had become a thriving community that included a diverse list of businesses that slowly began to expand away from the cross roads of town.

Fig. 2.12 *Corbette's Dairy, ca. 1940's – 1950's*
Corbette A. LeBlanc, owner

Fig. 2.13 *LeBlanc's Rice Mill*
Julian LeBlanc, owner

Fig. 2.14 *Whole families participated in farming. Children regularly committed to chores and family business after school. (Billy and Dorothy Steen, Iota, La.)*

25

In the first quarter of this century, rice had become king of the crops and the construction of the Hunter Canal and its branches served multiple purposes. The Hunter Canal Company and Acadia-Vermilion Rice Irrigation Company (AVRICO) pumped water from Bayou Vermilion and the Mermentau River into canals that fed thousands of acres of rice within and around Maurice. For a period of time, any flat land that was not used for grazing was dedicated to rice. Large landowners paid the canal company for delivery of water to their farms. Many rice farmers like Jill and Esson Picard, who leased several hundred acres, paid a percentage to the canal company and to the landowners, and still managed to make a profit on their harvest. Rice was planted in Maurice as close as the land across Maurice Avenue from Soop's Restaurant.

The Hunter Canal brought other benefits to area residents and served as a favored fishing and swimming place. But today, on the periphery of the city limits, only some of the old earthen canal walls are still visible after rice irrigation disappeared from the town. The remaining narrow strips of land, formed by rights-of-way of the old canals, are marketed as commercial and residential lots.

Fig. 2.15 Yvonne *"Donnie" Villien.*   ***Fig. 2.16*** *Alberta "Berta" Villien.*

Hunter Canal was part of a 400 mile system of rice irrigation channels in Vermilion Parish. Shown here at Maurice is the main channel running east-west approximately 20 miles. Large pumps carried water from the Bayou Vermilion at Milton.

Livestock played an important role in local economy. Beginning in the earliest days, beef cattle produced the most income. Getting cattle to market was difficult until improved roads came about in the 1930s. Cattle were driven many miles to market. The Villien, Broussard, LeBlanc and Trahan families of Maurice, to name a few, turned a modest profit from beef and dairy cattle. Most farms of the area were small in size but typically diversified. Black Angus cattle were the mainstay of the cattle industry on the Villien farm for many years.

The Villien herds were large enough that practically every member of the family owned their own brand. The following had registered brands: Mrs. Maurice Villien, IJV (transferred to Alfred Villien), J.A. Villien, IVI, Jacques C. Villien, JCV, Maude G. Villien, ħ, and Paul O. Villien, 9b.

Dr. J.A. Villien had one of the largest farms in the area. His home and farm was a modestly planned estate and a focal point of the community. James "Jack" Cyr Villien was the oldest son of Dr. Joseph A. and Octavia Broussard Villien. Jack was born in 1898 and married Rachel Martin of Carencro. He was very active in the Farm Bureau organization and served as vice-president of the Louisiana State Farm Bureau and an asset to local farmers. Jack and Rachel built a home adjacent to his father's and managed Dr. Villien's farming business until his death in 1962. George Carroll Villien, seventh son of Dr. Joseph A. and Annette Maude Gaidry Villien, succeeded Jack and managed the farm until his death in 1979.

The importance of water to agriculture is paramount; however, water came to Maurice in another way than by intentional irrigation. The Floods of 1927 and 1943 had devastating effects on homes, businesses and farmland. An interruption in sowing or harvesting of crops equated to loss of an entire year of income, in some cases, forced some small farmers to exit farming altogether. During the flood supplies were brought to Maurice by boat, wagon or large vehicle. In many areas around Maurice the flood waters were only inches deep but it was enough to cause overwhelming damage.

Fig. 2.17

March 13, 1943, the only access to Maurice was by large vehicle or boat. Bus service continued to operate along the poorly marked and flooded roadway. Families resorted to pirogue or bateau for access to higher ground. Louis and Wallace Broussard shown here departing Maurice for supplies in Lafayette.

Fig. 2.18

Fig. 2.19

Fig. 2.20

Fig. 2.21 Businesses throughout the village were completely surrounded by flood waters on March 13, 1943. Buildings in mid-town Maurice near the corner of John Street and Maurice Avenue were accessible by boat or large vehicles.

Blacksmiths

Farmers around Maurice relied greatly on the skill of blacksmiths, a trade that was considered by some to be an engineer of their day. In Maurice farmers relied on dependable blacksmiths. Two blacksmith shops were good competition for fashioning iron wagon rims, repairing farm implements, tools, and horse shoes. The forge and anvil of Abraham and Saul Broussard were in one shop and Aubrey Dronet in another. These were remembered as the best blacksmiths between Lafayette and Abbeville. Claude Broussard of Maurice recalled Saul's abilities to repair or make anything you needed from his blacksmith shop. Broussard's blacksmith shop was located behind Dr. Mouton's office and west of present day Ray's Convenience Store. Dronet's blacksmith shop was on the northwest corner of John Street and State Street.

Businesses of the Twenties

Around 1921, Dr. Villien built a new office in front of his home at the corner of State Street and West Joseph, the adjacent pecan grove was also planted at that time. His old office was relocated further north on Maurice Avenue, to become a grocery store – saloon – pool hall, all-in-one.

Jean-Maurice Villien, Jr. "T-N'oncle", brother of Dr. J. A. Villien, operated a saloon near the southwest corner of Maurice Avenue and Lafayette Street (Indian Bayou Road). The structure later became Gulley's Drugstore. This building contained two businesses. The drugstore occupied the north half of the building and Dr. Carroll J. Mouton's medical office was in the south half of the building. A. Bruce Mouton purchased the drugstore business ca. 1928 and continued the only drugstore in Maurice until 1973.

Also in 1921, Dr. Villien founded the Bank of Maurice, an independent financial institution. The bank was affected by the 1929 stock market crash and closed temporarily. It reopened in 1933 after the depression and was reorganized under ownership of the Bank of Abbeville and Trust Company – Maurice Branch.

Fig. 2.22 *Bank of Maurice, established 1921. The Bank of Abbeville purchased the building in circa 1932.*

Fig. 2.23 *Philip E. Trahan, Teller (L) and Dr. J.A. Villien, Manager (R). Bank of Abbeville, Maurice Branch*

Fig. 2.24 *Sanborn Map, a 1921 timepiece reveals bygone locations of general merchandise stores, black smith shops, offices, the cotton gin, a public school, a church and a bank.*

Fig. 2.25 Bank of Abbeville and Trust, ca. 1963 (L - R) Corbette LeBlanc, Joseph A. Villien, Jr. and Claude J. Broussard.

Fig. 2.26 A. Bruce Mouton, owner of the Maurice Drug Store. Mr. Mouton purchased the drug store in ca. 1928. This photo was taken in June 1970.

Felix Nugent established a bar on Maurice Avenue in 1927. Shortly after opening the City Bar, Cyprien Trahan and his son, Ernest Trahan, purchased and continued the business under the same name. In the 1930s it became one of the most popular watering holes in Vermilion Parish. Following their deaths, Ernest Charles "Charlie" Trahan and his son, Matthew, continued operation of the business. Many Cajuns considered the City Bar as home of Boo-ray "bourré," a card game indigenous to Cajun country. Patrons know it to be where the rules of the game were written. The City Bar, a landmark of the region and a place of worldwide notoriety, has remained in continuous operation since it opened.

Fig. 2.27 City Bar – (L-R) Ernest Trahan, Gladu Montet, C.E."Charlie" Trahan and Thear Simon.

30

Albert A. Villien clerked at his father's store, Villien Brothers before opening his own business in 1923. Albert established the Maurice Garage which was continued by Otto Comeaux in 1957 and then by Warren Rost (current Chief of Police) until 1976. Albert became employed at Wood Motors, then Bay City Motors in Abbeville until he retired.

Fig. 2.28 Maurice Garage, founded in 1923 by Albert A. Villien

Fig. 2.29 Comeaux's Bar, established ca. 1940's

Lannes Comeaux owned a small grocery store which was a part of his home. The store was located on the corner of John and State Street, the site of the first Maurice School. In 1946, Lannes closed the grocery business and went to work with his uncle Mayo Comeaux who established Comeaux's Bar. Lannes later took over management of the bar with his son, Curtis Comeaux. The original building was owned by Agnues Comeaux and no longer exists but was replaced by the present cinder block building and to this day is still owned by the Comeaux family. The name of the bar was later changed to Como's Bar managed by Rodney Broussard, Sammy Picard and Douglas Picard. The building later became Doug's Main Street Bar and presently is named The Booze Barn.

Enterprises of the Thirties and Forties

The E. G. Trahan office building first served as Port Broussard's Shell service station operated by Elphege "Port" and Gladys Broussard. Elphege was a foster child of Ernest and Laura Trahan. The building became the post office in the mid-1940's. Located on the south side of the service station (northeast corner of Maurice Avenue and Lafayette Street) was T-Coon's Bar, owned by Odeus "Coon" Luquette. The bar ceased operation prior to 1948. About the same time, Savy "Coon" Duhon operated Coon's Service Station on the west side of Maurice Avenue north of Dr. Harold Trahan's former home. The business was subsequently bought by Edward "Sport" Hebert and called Sport's Auto Repair.

Once again local economy was strengthened by a Broussard family business when Ducré Broussard opened a small business that was a combination hardware, appliance and auto parts business. Ducré and Olive Broussard opened Dixie Auto-Lec around the mid-1940s. The store was located on the southwest corner of Maurice Avenue and West Lafayette Street. Ducré died in 1951, his oldest son, Fred, continued to run the business until 1957.

African-American Businesses

The African-American families of Maurice, beginning with its early settlers of Catalon and Chargois contributed greatly to development of the community. In 1873, Arvillien and Felicia Catalon homesteaded a quarter section of land west of Maurice. Dorice [sic] Catalon was instrumental in founding the first Catholic Church for Blacks, St. Joseph Church. Many of the Catalon and Chargois family worked at local farms and businesses in Maurice

Fig. 2.30 *Eldridge "Son" Catalon, ca. 1960's. Catalon Grocery was in business from 1947 to 1985*

32

In 1947, Eldridge "Son" Catalon and his wife, Emma, established the first Black owned business in Maurice. Catalon Grocery was an ordinary country store that consisted of the usual inventory of daily family needs. The store was established on property Eldridge inherited from his father, Dorice Catalon, during a period when segregation was commonplace and colored people were proud to call Catalon's Store their own. The grocery continued operation until 1985.

The Catalon name first appeared on the Land Grant documents in 1860 and considered one of the first families in Maurice. From the time of their arrival, many family members have been active in business and community affairs. Since nineteen seventy-four there has been a Catalon family member on the Maurice Board of Aldermen. Paul Catalon served on the board for approximately thirty years until his death in 2005. His son, Troy, filled the vacancy plus one term until 2011. In January 2011 Troy's sister, Phyllis Catalon, filled the vacancy after Troy completed his term.

Fig. 2.31   *Catalon Grocery – Eldridge and Emma Catalon established a country grocery store and from its humble beginnings, the business prevailed as a service to the community for nearly forty years.*

Black folks from Vermilion, Lafayette and Iberia Parishes patronized a popular little bar over in Maurice. On Friday and Saturday nights people came from far and wide for a good time. In the nineteen forties the Chargois brothers owned a bar on the north side of Maurice named "The Plantation Bar." Caesair [sic] Chargois did not agree with his brothers about managing the bar so he walked away and built his own, the Hidden Village Lounge. Cesair and Lena Chargois started the little bar in a wood framed building without electric lights and their living quarters at the rear of the building. Eventually electric lights replaced the lanterns and good times rolled until closure in 2009.

Public Services

Fig. 3.1 *Handwritten Proclamation for the Village of Maurice, December 27, 1911. The proclamation declared the village incorporated, defined its limits and fixed its name as the "Village of Maurice".*

Public Services

3

Proclamation

Jean-Maurice Villien envisioned building a small city and ultimately succeeded at laying the foundation. At the outset, the fundamental structure and functions of government were established by residents of Mauriceville. Two-thirds of qualified voters of the unincorporated community of Mauriceville passed a referendum, incorporating a two square mile area as the Village of Maurice. On December 27, 1911, by his seal of approval, Jared Y. Sanders, Governor of Louisiana certified the proclamation set forth by the people of Maurice.

Village records made no mention of fanfare or celebration regarding the proclamation. The first meeting of the Board of Aldermen, recorded into the minute book on January 2, 1912, that it was a "special session". The first aldermen were Erast Broussard, Hilaire D. Broussard, H.A. Bacque; and Secretary Pro Tem Cyprien D. Trahan. The first assembly of the board appointed Dr. Joseph A. Villien, mayor.

The Board of Aldermen first held regular public meetings in the Maurice School until 1920. Subsequently, the meetings were in the Woodmen of the World Hall on Maurice Avenue and in the Ernest G. Trahan office building from 1950 to 1966, and again in the Woodmen of the World Hall from 1966 to 1969. A place that villagers could finally call City Hall was established fifty-eight years after incorporation. The first fire station located at 405 Lastie Avenue was renovated in 1969 and converted to become the City Hall.

Streets and Roads

Public streets were at the forefront of municipal discussions since the first right-of-ways were dedicated in 1911. Beyond initial grading of roads, little had been done in the form of improvements and extensions until 1926. In that year Albert Street and Corine Street were extended. The two streets and the new Maurice High School were choreographed to open within the same year. Albert Street was opened to the public from Lafayette Street to Corine Street and Corine Street was extended from Maurice Avenue to Albert Street.

Politicians worked hard to keep the Village of Maurice connected. Roadways were the subject of debate in two separate eras of local past. The future course of development and the history of the town may have hinged on decisions that affected Maurice Avenue on both occasions. In 1921 and again in 1975 the mayor and Board of Aldermen grappled with Louisiana State authorities about designation of a proposed state highway route between Lafayette and Abbeville.

In 1921 State administrators were juggling options of proposed routes located on either side of the Vermilion Bayou. On September 10, 1921, Mayor Joseph A. Villien and Aldermen Felix Nugent, J.A. Dartez and Elie Vincent, adopted a resolution for presentation to the Louisiana State Legislature. A showing of Dr. Joseph Villien, Dr. Carroll Mouton, Cyprien D. Trahan and Father Pierre M. Gruel attended the legislative session in Baton Rouge and presented arguments and alternatives for the alignment of the impending highway. Their persistence was most likely the linchpin to the legislature's approval of the west side route. The State also began maintaining and numbering highway routes in 1921. The road from Abbeville to Lafayette became a primary state highway and was first numbered as Louisiana Highway 43 and later became U.S. Highway 167. Pavement of the road was not completed until 1937.

Fig. 3.2 Newly paved Maurice Avenue was a welcomed improvement for buggies, automobiles, businesses and residents. Mrs. Ada Broussard looks on from her front porch at a passing buggy and enjoying a dust-free ride on the concrete roadway. The Maurice Garage is shown at the right of the photograph.

Louisiana, particularly in this region, had a reputation for having the worst roads. Promises by Governors O.K. Allen and Richard W. Leche of paving the road from Lafayette to Abbeville had still not yet been completed by January 1937. The meandering and deeply rutted gravel road was under construction. Paving of Louisiana Highway 43 from Abbeville to Maurice was not finished until the latter part of 1937. The paved portion of Maurice Avenue terminated at its intersection with Vincent Road, at the north end of town. The primary route from Maurice to Lafayette continued as gravel surface that headed east along Vincent Road then north on Andre Avenue and crossed Coulee Ile des Cannes into Lafayette Parish.

36

The second time that local roads became the forefront of political debate was in 1975. Mayor Corbette LeBlanc may have single-handedly changed the course of history in Maurice when Louisiana state officials and the Department of Transportation were seriously planning to build a by-pass that would circumnavigate Maurice altogether. Mayor LeBlanc would not tolerate such a consideration and worked diligently in keeping the road alignment as it is, through the center of Maurice. In lieu of a by-pass, Mayor LeBlanc convinced Governor Edwin Edwards to four-lane Maurice Avenue as the main thoroughfare and to abandon the idea of an alternate route. The alternate roadway may have changed life in Maurice as we know it today.

Early Utilities
Little evidence exists today that telegraph was in operation in Maurice around the 1910s and 20s. Though, a early photograph of Father Louis Laroche, circa 1910 – 1920, provided a glimpse of a telegraph pole in the background of the photograph. The pole was located along Maurice Avenue (west side) near the home of Jean Villien. Telegraph, the communication utility, born some sixty years prior to this photograph, had finally arrived in Maurice a mere two decades before telephone service. The telegraph office in Maurice was in the postal office at Villien Brothers store.

Right-of-ways for utilities also became a political topic as early as 1928, though not as hotly debated as road right-of-ways. Maurice Board of Aldermen Bruce Mouton, Saul Broussard and John Villien approved the first franchise to J.C. Bertrand of Lafayette the use of public right of ways for running electric lines within Maurice in 1928. Electricity had been in service at Lafayette since 1897 but smaller towns like Scott and Maurice were not fully served until the 1920's. Around 1930, the first radio appeared in Maurice in the home of Albert Villien. In 1929 the board approved another resolution that eased progress for expansion of electric service to the rest of the community. The board exempted Gulf States Utilities from paying taxes on construction of utilities. But it was not until March 1938 when the town entered into its first contract with Gulf States Utilities to install city-owned electric street lights. The community of Maurice had finally come of age as street lights were added a few at a time.

Back in the early 1920s, electricity was scarce in many rural Louisiana areas. Electric lines in Maurice and other small communities had not yet been constructed. Residents in Maurice relied on coal oil or calcium carbide generators as a source of fuel for lanterns and gas lamps. More importantly, the matter of perishable foods relied on refrigeration and electricity was needed to make ice. For a period of time, the only company producing electricity was Central Louisiana Ice & Electric in Bunkie, later known as CLECO. Abraham Broussard was granted a permit in 1939 to operate the first ice depot in Maurice. Ice houses sold ice by the block and it was delivered by ice wagons to homes.

Telephones were gradually making debut in Louisiana rural areas during the 1940s. The Maurice Board of Aldermen approved the first permit for Southern Bell Telephone and Telegraph Company to install and operate equipment in 1946. The first telephones were located in Villien Brothers Store, the bank, the school and in the homes of Dr. J. A. Villien, Albert Villien and Adonis Picard. The telephone became a prominent feature wherever it was installed. A sign of the times was the party-line which consisted of eight telephones sharing one line. A native son of Maurice, Dr. Lastie M. Villien, made history in a nearby south Louisiana town on October 1, 1949 when he received the first dial phone call in Jeanerette from Mr. L. Thornton.

World War II

During World War II, the Village of Maurice contributed its share to protecting what the United States War Department considered as the designated *Critical Defense Area*. Maurice was part of a designated area important to national security and in January 1943 the board of aldermen approved regulations necessary for protection of the area and its citizens. A detailed black out ordinance controlled every aspect of lighting in Maurice for the

Fig. 3.3 Dr. Lastie Villien received the first dialed telephone call in Jeanerette in 1949.

duration of the war. A lookout tower was constructed and manned by volunteers to be on the look-out for enemy aircraft. Volunteers also collected a mountain of scrap metal for the war effort. The scrap pile was located on the school ground and was nearly as high as the lookout tower.

There were many in Maurice who participated in making the town a safer place during the war. Men who did not enlist into the armed forces served in the Louisiana State Guard. The 156 Infantry was inducted into federal service from 1940 to 1946 and headquartered in Lafayette.

Fig. 3.4 Thear Simon and Ducré Broussard in uniform of the Louisiana State Guard, Maurice School in background.

38

Few people today are aware that from 1943 to 1945, Maurice had its own army airfield. Maurice Field Auxiliary No.3 was one of Lafayette Municipal Airport's four support fields which provided Contract Pilot School (CPS) training for the AAF and V-12 Program. Duson, Broussard, and Youngsville also had airfields. The United States War Department included Maurice in a critical defense zone. The old airfield, now farmland, is still referenced as the "Maurice airport." The hundred acre site was part of the Villien family estate located on the east side of Highway 167 and south of Coulee Ile des Cannes.

Fred Villien, a native of Maurice, was in pilot training at Brooks Field in Texas during the war. Fred "Freddie" Villien, Jr. spoke of the excitement that was created when his father came home to Maurice. Before coming home on furlough, he would send a telegram to his home in Maurice and someone notified the Maurice School so that all the children could come to see the plane when it approached the Maurice airport. Seeing an Army aircraft piloted by a Maurice native was a big deal in those days.

Pedestrian Access
In years past, business owners, civic leaders and church leaders often expressed their interest in helping one another within the community. In a period before servitudes and right-of-ways dedicated for sidewalks, almost every entity or establishment provided pedestrian walkways for convenience. In a wet climate such as the South, board-walks were commonplace and practically necessary. A working relationship on community projects was almost perpetual between church, school and village leaders, as though there was no separation between church and state. It was not unheard of, for example, to find combined effort to build board-walks or hold fund raisers and gatherings for school and church. Nor was it rare for public funds to be used on church and other private properties.

Pedestrian access between business, church and school proved to be important to civic leaders and property owners alike. In those early years when sidewalks were built of wood, maintenance was a continual problem and town officials constantly battled deteriorating lumber and destruction from horses and wagons. There was great concern about riding horses on sidewalks, important enough that it was the second ordinance written into law in 1912.

Fig. 3.5 (L-R) John Broussard, Doris Broussard, Margaret Hebert Gremillion, Louise Dartez Broussard, Pat Broussard Langlinais, Alice Broussard Schroder and Gladys Broussard Trahan enjoying the concrete pedestrian walk along Maurice Avenue.

Years later, land owners worked together in 1949 in an effort to dedicate right-of-way for construction of cement sidewalks. The wooden sidewalks proved expensive and the cost of construction of cement sidewalks was made affordable because fifteen property owners on the west side and eight on the east side of Maurice Avenue committed to pay half of construction costs in addition to donating right-of-way. One of the last civic projects under Mayor Carroll J. Mouton's administration was implementation of his plan for more than three thousand feet of sidewalk along Maurice Avenue.

Bicentennial Welcome

Residents of Maurice are people of pride and politeness. Their warm and unforgotten cultural hospitality and civic duty was displayed when they welcomed the authentic wagon train commemorating the nation's bicentennial of 1976. The wagon train camped in Crowley the night before arriving in Maurice. The Maurice Jaycees, as a public service project, arranged for the wagon train to come through Vermilion Parish and Maurice. They continued on through Milton and Youngsville and on up to Valley Forge arriving there for the July 4th, 1976 national celebration.

Fig. 3.6 Bicentennial Wagon Train Pilgrimage, 1976. In June 1975 the Bicentennial Wagon Train Pilgrimage started in Blaine, Washington and ended on July 4, 1976 in Valley Forge, Pennsylvania. Each state was provided a Conestoga or Prairie Schooner Wagon by the Pilgrimage and joined the caravan as it passed through the state.

40

Seven Administrators
Seven chief administrators served during the first century of Maurice history.

Fig. 3.7 *First Mayor, Dr. J.A. Villien, Sr., was the son of Jean-Maurice Villien, founder of the Village of Maurice.*

Fig. 3.8 *Second Mayor, Dr. Carroll J. Mouton, was born in 1899 and was a native of Lafayette.*

Fig. 3.9 *Third Mayor, Dr. Harold G. Trahan, Sr., was elected in 1949. Dr. Trahan was a native of Maurice and served as mayor from 1949 to 1962.*

Fig. 3.10 *Fourth Mayor, Corbette A. LeBlanc, Sr., was a native of Vermilion Parish and served as mayor from 1962 to 1982.*

Fig. 3.11 *Fifth Mayor, Barbara Landry Picard, was a native of Delcambre. She is the daughter of Ollie and Bernadette Landry of Delcambre.*

Fig. 3.12 *Sixth Mayor, Robert H. "Bob" Ferguson, was born 1946 and is a native of Maurice. He is the son of Edward and Jeanne Ferguson of Maurice.*

Fig. 3.13 *Seventh Mayor, Wayne Theriot, is a native of Abbeville and has been a resident of Maurice since 1979. Wayne married Marlene Broussard, a teacher at Cecil Picard Elementary.*

Louisiana Cleanest City

The community of Maurice entered the statewide "Cleanest City Contest" in 1989. The Maurice Jaycees, under the leadership of Blaire Hebert, led an intense clean-up campaign with local residents. The community placed first in Category "A" in District III then placed second in state.

Again in April 1990 Maurice entered the "Cleanest City Contest" but this time claimed first place in Louisiana. The Jaycees again spearheaded the campaign with the help of residents, neighbors, churches, schools and Police Juror Harry Broussard.

Fig. 3.14 *The Village of Maurice did not have a City Hall until the town purchased the old Maurice Volunteer Fire Station and renovated the building in 1969.*

Infrastructure and Public Works

The June 1954 election was the first time in village history that a voting machine was used by voters. Elected officials were Mayor Harold G. Trahan, Aldermen Elix Hebert, Corbette A. LeBlanc and Edward W. Hebert. One of Mayor Trahan's first official acts was approval of a contract with United Gas Corporation for construction of natural gas pipelines in Maurice. Gas service lines were completed by 1953. Before Mayor Trahan left office, he was instrumental in achieving a hard surface pavement program for all of the streets. During the nineteen fifties village leaders relieved the Vermilion Parish Police Jury of maintenance obligations for some of the local streets. Among the list of streets that were hard surfaced under a Police Jury paving project and then turned over to the town were: Lafayette, John, Opta, Church, Broussard, Joseph and Saint Albert Street.

Village Aldermen approved three new public streets during the nineteen sixties. Terry Street, Sammy Lane and an extension of Albert Street to East Lafayette Street. Mayor Corbette LeBlanc and aldermen successfully completed a street paving program. Claude Breaux, Street Commissioner, spearheaded acquisition of a new Leach rear-loader compactor garbage truck which was a huge advancement to city-wide maintenance of sanitary conditions. Herbert Norman was hired as garbage collector and in 1969 the village assessed residents two dollars per month for once a week pickup.

Improvements to Maurice infrastructure came slowly until Mayor Corbette LeBlanc secured federal funds for brick and mortar improvements. In 1974, with cooperation from aldermen and U.S. Representative John Breaux, Senators Russell B. Long and J. Bennett Johnston, Mayor LeBlanc secured federal grants from the Department of Housing and Urban Development in excess of two hundred twenty-five thousand dollars for upgrades to wastewater treatment, potable water systems and a water tower.

Fig. 3.15
Maurice Department of Water

Barbara Picard became the fifth mayor and first woman to serve as mayor. In 1982 she spearheaded several public works projects, including resurfacing of all the village streets. Perhaps some of her most significant projects included construction of the one hundred fifty foot high water tower and the water system upgrade in 1993. In 1994 she again pushed through street overlay and road reconstruction projects. With the help of federal grant money in 1999 a significant sewer treatment facility upgrade was made and sewer lines were extended.

Mayor Bob Ferguson led the expansion and upgrade project to completion for the water treatment plant started in 2006. Ferguson also assured sewer line extensions in areas north and south of town. Overall municipal water pressure was increased which provided improved fire protection and potable water pressure to homes. Mayor Ferguson was instrumental and

Fig. 3.16 *Lapel Pens of the Village of Maurice*

successful in attaining improved subdivision standards which provided for wider streets, better drainage and pedestrian access. During Ferguson's last year in office he paved the way for a 3.4 million dollar sewer improvement upgrade which was slated for construction in 2010.

In 1989 Maurice was declared one of the cleanest cities in Louisiana. In its classification of towns with a population of less than 1,500, Maurice was awarded first place in District III and second place in the state of Louisiana.

Police Protection

Police Chief Warren Rost is the thirteenth marshal and has served longer than any of his predecessors. After twenty-nine years on the force, he considers the village to be a very safe place to live. Chief Rost described Maurice as a "small closely-knit community who are watching out for each other. Neighborhood Watch existed before the popular concept of Neighborhood Watch came about." The 2010 annual budget for the police division was approximately $225,000.00. The division was staffed by six officers and was equipped with the latest technology including six patrol cars with built-in laptop computers, cameras and speed detection equipment.

Fig. 3.17 Mayor and Aldermen in 2002 (L – R) Paul Catalon, Lee Wood, Mayor Barbara Picard, Mary Hebert and Marlene B. Theriot

Fig. 3.18 The Village of Maurice Police Department

Vermilion Parish Library – Maurice Branch

The Maurice Library was first located at Maurice Elementary School. In the 1970's the library moved into a house near the corner of Albert and E. Joseph Street. In 1976 it moved to the present location on the southeast corner of E. Joseph and Maurice Avenue. Since 1944 the library has had nine librarians. The current librarian, Cheryl Bergeron, arrived in 1994. Charlotte Trosclair is Director of the Vermilion Parish Library, Maurice Branch.

Fig. 3.19 Vermilion Parish Library System, Maurice Branch. (Located on the southeast corner of Joseph Street and Maurice Avenue)

45

Maurice Park

In 1967 Vermilion Parish Sheriff, Euda Delcambre, donated recreational equipment for the Maurice baseball field. There were no public parks in Maurice before 1983 and the lone recreational area was privately maintained. Recreation was confined to available facilities either at the Maurice High School campus or a two and a half acre area located on church property on the corner of Maurice Avenue and Joseph Street. St. Alphonsus Church allowed the Little League Baseball team use of this site for many years. This quadrant of the church property was the site of the first St. Alphonsus Church Hall.

Fig. 3.20 Maurice Park Dedication Ceremony, 1983. (L-R) Elinor Craven, Sammy Theriot, Cecil Picard, Margaret Wynne, Jennifer Laughlin, Barbara Picard and Corbette LeBlanc.

Since 1975 the civic leaders and residents worked tirelessly toward building a new public park on East Lafayette Street. In April 1981, Mayor Corbette LeBlanc and Willie Broussard were successful in obtaining approval from the town council for the new facility. The 13.5 acre park received a $100,000 grant from the Louisiana Department of Transportation and a donation from the family of Arline Villien Wynne. Arline Villien Wynne was a great-granddaughter of Jean-Maurice Villien.

Maurice Park was completed after months of planning and negotiating details. A ribbon cutting and dedication ceremony was held on Sunday June 29, 1983 at the new park. The officiates who cut the ceremonial ribbon were: Elinor Craven, State Representative Sammy Theriot, State Senator Cecil Picard, Margaret Wynne, Jennifer Laughlin, Mayor Barbara Picard and former Mayor Corbette LeBlanc. Later that year the Board of Aldermen appointed a four member Park and Recreation Commission to oversee park operations.

Fig. 3.21 Little League Baseball Park 1970. St. Alphonsus Catholic Church allowed the Maurice Little League Baseball team use of a vacant field adjacent to the church.

46

Post Office

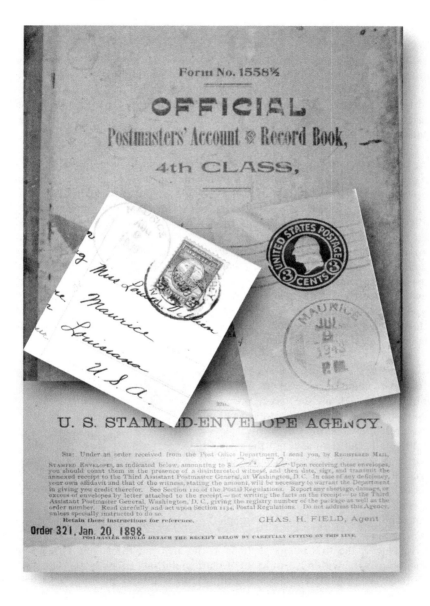

Fig. 4.1 *Maurice Postmarks, Maurice, Louisiana*

Post Office

4

Early Mail Delivery

Prior to 1895 people of Broussard Cove traveled to Abbeville, Lafayette or Milton to obtain their mail. Delivery of mail was brought by way of rail to Lafayette and Abbeville and by schooner on the Vermilion Bayou to Milton. An increase in area population and demand for improved mail service gave reason for Jean-Maurice Villien to file application to establish a post office at Mauriceville.

The application was filed within a year after opening his store on Maurice Avenue and culminated with establishment of a U.S. Post Office on September 19, 1895, inside of Mr. Villien's store. Broussard Cove had approximately one thousand population and Mauriceville, as it was locally called, consisted of a population of fifty. When the Postal Service requested that Mr. Villien provide a name for the post office and postmark, he made it simple and gave the name that most people called him, "Maurice." The combination of a post office and a general store in one building made good business sense and a great gathering place for locals to catch-up on the latest news. By the turn of the century people received newspapers and magazines by mail, giving local farmers and residents a new source of educational information. The two businesses contributed, in part, to the humble beginnings of the Village of Maurice.

Delivery of mail to the Maurice post office was made by way of horseback or mail wagon from the larger postal depots of Abbeville or Lafayette. Mail was relatively slow to arrive in Mauriceville but mail was not the only source of communication around the turn of the century. Lafayette and Abbeville newspapers were very capable in providing current events on state and national affairs. Telegraph lines had crossed the region as early as

Fig. 4.2 First post office was located within Le Magasin à Maurice.

1875. One of the first telegraph lines in the area ran from New Orleans to Beaumont and within a mile of Mauriceville at Broussard's Crossing (Milton). Telegraph came into service in Maurice around the mid-1920s with a telegraph receiver established in the post office at Villien Brothers Store.

Postmasters

Dr. Joseph A. Villien took over as the second postmaster after his father died in 1902. Dr. Villien's office and his father's store were adjacent buildings that fronted on Maurice Avenue. Villien Brothers store was constructed on the corner of Maurice Avenue and Church Street around 1916 and the post office was moved from Maurice's old store into the Villien Brothers store. Dr. Villien served as postmaster from 1902 to 1913. In 1913, Dr. Villien relinquished the postmaster's position and Cyprien D. Trahan, an employee of Villien Brothers, took over as postmaster.

Later the post office was moved to the Ernest G. Trahan office building. Cyprien D. Trahan continued to serve as postmaster until 1946 when Robert "Bob" L. Trahan was hired as his replacement. Bob Trahan served as postmaster from 1946 to 1982.

Fig. 4.3 *United States Post Office.   E.G. Trahan office building on Maurice Avenue, C.A. LeBlanc (L) and E.C. "Charlie" Trahan (R).*

The Ernest G. Trahan building first served as a service station. When the building was converted to a post office, it also served as the bus depot for the Teche Greyhound and LaPorte bus lines. In addition to serving the general public, the commercial bus lines were means of daily transportation for students attending schools in Lafayette or Abbeville. Mary Beth Trahan Dupuis, a daughter of Postmaster Bob Trahan, recalled riding one of the bus lines to school. When in grade school she rode the bus to and from school in Abbeville. She was quite amused by her faux pas on one occasion when she forgot to exit the bus at the post office in Maurice. Mr. Bob, her dad the postmaster, ran out of the post office and chased the bus until it stopped to let her off. The amusing story of the postmaster chasing a bus down the highway is an example of what daily life was like around the post office. Until the building was demolished, the interior post office walls bare markings of Mr. Bob's children growth and height record penciled on his office wall.

Fig. 4.4   *Robert "Bob" Trahan, Postmaster*

Fig. 4.5   *Post Office dedication plaque, 1982*

The present post office building on John Street was constructed in 1982 by the U.S. Postal Service. Postmasters since 1982 were Jessie J. Champagne, Dale Dooley, Calvin Arrington and Paul Thibodeaux.

Fig. 4.6 *United States Post Office on John Street in 2011*

Fire Department

Fig. 5.1 *Maurice Volunteer Fire Apparatus No. 73*

Fire Department

5

Origin of the Department

A firefighter's goal is to protect life and property. In February 1967 citizens of Maurice banned together and took it upon themselves to organize an all volunteer fire department after witnessing the loss of two local homes. In order to accomplish their goal, the members of Maurice Volunteer Fire Department agreed on a pact to function as a team, not an organization of individuals. The founding members adopted a heart-felt motto, "*We volunteer because we care*".

Fig. 5.2 *The first Maurice Volunteer Fire Department station was located on Lastie Avenue in 1967.*

The origin of the department is credited to those who called the first meeting. Wallace Broussard, Golden Landry, Fidney Trahan and Lester Gauthier printed flyers, posted notices and went door-to-door and announced the first meeting for February 2, 1967. That meeting was held in the Maurice High School Gym, ironically in the location that would later become the department's largest and most dangerous fire in its history.

Fig. 5.3 *The current Maurice Volunteer Fire Department station is located on Chief H. Fred Broussard Avenue (formerly State Street.)*

Fig. 5.4 *First Fire Truck*

The first administrative officers were elected in February 1967 in a community meeting of more than one hundred people. The elected officers were: Carroll Comeaux, President; Paul Ray Landry, First Vice-President; Wallace Broussard, Second Vice-President; Golden Landry, Secretary; Claude

Broussard, Treasurer; A. Bruce Mouton, Board Member; and Johnny Picard, Board Member

Fourteen firemen were trained at Louisiana State University in Baton Rouge by May 1967. Although, the department did not have a truck and the town did not have a water system, a program was started to educate non-believers that fires could be extinguished from a portable tank. The first truck was delivered one year later.

By August 1967 the first fire fighting officers were elected: H. Fred Broussard, Fire Chief; Will Broussard, First Assistant Chief; Nason Trahan, Second Assistant Chief; Sammy Picard, First Captain; Perry Stelly, Second Captain; and Ray Broussard, Traffic Marshal.

By late 1967 the Fire Department had become an important community asset and joined the ranks of school and church. It became another focal point in the community that enlisted interest and commitment from all of the residents in the area. Fund raisers began to grow larger and included barbeques, auctions, dances and trail rides.

In 1976 area voters approved a proposal by the Vermilion Parish Police Jury for funding of solid waste, mosquito and fire protection programs. The funding provided for the new Vermilion Fire Protection Association of five volunteer fire departments. Since that association began, Carroll Comeaux of Maurice, served one year, Fred Broussard served two years and Matthew Trahan served as president for twelve years.

Fig. 5.5 *Fire Apparatus Logos painted on each truck*

In 1968, a unique method of calling firemen for emergencies was installing dedicated telephones throughout the community in businesses and homes for emergency alert with a uniform protocol. Seven phones were installed: Fred's Plumbing, City Bar, Wills I.G., Dudley Trahan's home, Fred Broussard's home, Dallas Landry's home and Willie Broussard's home.

During the first ten years the department's response area included parts of Lafayette and Milton. The area has since been reduced due to other fire departments established in those areas.

The department's response to significant incidents between 1967 and 2011 included callouts to: Maurice High School, Texaco Plant, Meaux Elementary, E. Broussard High School, Hebert brothers (Leonard and Timmy Hebert plane crash), Liberty Rice Mill, Erath Middle School and St. Mary Magdalen Catholic Church.

Fig. 5.6 *Meaux High School Fire, April 1994*

In 1995 the department received a grant from the village of Maurice for a pumper truck. After receiving the new truck, a tradition was initiated by the department for naming units after firemen who contributed in a significant way to the community and the fire department. The first pumper truck was named "Big Fred" after Chief H. Fred Broussard; the second, "Mr. Carroll" was the F550 mini pumper after Carroll Comeaux; the third, "Chief Matt," a 2004 GMC 1500 gallon per minute pumper, was named for Chief Matthew Trahan; and the fourth, "Rod," the rescue-service unit was named in honor of Rod Broussard.

Fig. 5.7 *Fire Apparatus and Maurice VFD Seal*

Chief Mathew C. Trahan, Fire Chief in 2010, had 29 volunteer firemen to assist in emergencies. The department served an area much greater than the Village of Maurice and included an estimated population of 3,500.

A real life hero

Chief H. Fred Broussard was a real life hero. The founding member of the department was a dedicated friend, citizen and volunteer fireman who inspired more and more people to help others. One of the darkest days in the history of Maurice was in November 1999 when Fred died suddenly in the course of his job fighting an intense fire at Dale Broussard's service station south of Maurice.

Chief Broussard, was recognized and honored in 1999 by the National Volunteer Firefighters Council and the National Fallen Firefighters Foundation.

The National Fallen Firefighters Foundation memorialized Chief Broussard with the following inscription:

Fred, 69, Chief of the Maurice Volunteer Fire Department since its inception in 1967, died on November 18, 1999, after suffering a heart attack while fighting a tanker fire. Owner of a local plumbing and electric company, he was well known throughout the fire community. He served as President of the Louisiana Fire Chiefs Association and President of the Vermilion Fire Protection district."

Fig. 5.8 *H. Fred Broussard,*
Fire Chief

Fig. 5.9 *Memorial to*
Chief H. Fred Broussard

Property Insurance Affected

When the fire department was established in 1976 it was required to meet certain criteria according to a rating system established by Property Insurance Association of Louisiana. The purpose is to evaluate fire defenses and to establish property insurance rates. The Village of Maurice did not have a water system in place, therefore the department was rated ten, the lowest rank on a scale of one to ten. Through subsequent installation of a water system excellent record-keeping and fireman training, the department steadily improved its rating to seven in 1994 and to three by 2009. The Maurice Volunteer Fire Department in 2011 had in excess of a million dollars invested in five trucks and equipment and a five bay fire station valued at approximately two hundred thousand dollars.

Fig. 5.10 *We Volunteer Because We Care*

Mid-Century Trade

Fig. 6.1 *C.A. LeBlanc General Merchandise*

Mid-Century Trade
6

Attack on Business

In the years nearing the semicentennial of Maurice, the country village was enjoying its' quaint, tranquil and laid back atmosphere. Rarely was anyone in a rush or disturbed the peace. But on the gloomy and cool winters' day of Wednesday, February 17, 1954, there was a deadly attack on the very heart of business. Perhaps one of the most talked about regional events of the twentieth century occurred when a lone robber entered the bank in Maurice. The event became national attention when the Bank of Abbeville and Trust Company (formerly Bank of Maurice) robbery took place leaving behind spent cartridges and a trail of blood. The killer was on the run.

Kenneth C. Holdcraft of Lafayette, carried two pistols and a rifle into the bank. The only other person in the bank was the manager, 83 year old Dr. J.A. Villien. During the process of robbing the bank, Philip E. Trahan, the teller who had left the building, returned to the bank and saw what was happening. A physical scuffle ensued between all three men with shots fired by Holdcraft. During the scuffle, Holdcraft pulled his second pistol from his waist-belt. Holdcraft fired and killed Mr. Trahan instantly and seriously wounded Dr. Villien. Holdcraft went to the opened safe and grabbed over $15,000 then escaped in a getaway car. Maurice Police Chief Robert Dartez gave chase to the fleeing taxi but lost him between Maurice and Lafayette. Ophe Trahan, a local farmer, also gave chase as the robber fled but he too could not keep up with Holdcraft. Through a series of coincidental events, State Trooper, E.I. Guidry and Game Ranger, E.J. Cormier, recognized the speeding vehicle on a back road near the town of Broussard.

Holdcraft's vehicle was chased to an area near Parks called Cypress Island located between Breaux Bridge and St. Martinville. Lawmen, Lt. Edward C. Lyles, Troopers E.L. Guidry and D.D. Landry with Game Ranger E.J. Cormier of Lafayette Parish then chased after him as he crossed a cow pasture. Holdcraft and officers exchanged over thirty shots before the robber was killed. Another Lafayette man, Earl Clayton Randolph, was later implicated as an accomplice of Holdcraft.

Reverend A.O. Sigur, assistant chaplain at Southwestern Louisiana Institute Catholic Student Center, and Louis J. Michot, Sr. of Lafayette happened to be passing through Maurice immediately after and stopped to offer assistance when they saw the crowd gathered around at the bank. Father Sigur went into the bank and gave Last Rites to Mr. Trahan and to Dr. Villien.

Dr. Villien was rushed to Palms Hospital in Abbeville where Dr. Don Williams removed the bullet from his chest. Dr. Villien recovered from his chest wounds. Nearly six decades later, the horrific event, to this day, is talked about by folks throughout southwest Louisiana.

Authors note: *I was very young when my grandfather was shot in the Maurice bank robbery. I remembered his description of the tragic event on that February day. He recounted the holdup to my dad in French, he paused occasionally, explaining the happenings to me in English. As I touched his scars from the bullet wounds, I thought of him as a hero for putting his life on the line to protect the bank and everyone's money.*

Fig. 6.2
Outlaw Kenneth C. Holdcraft was killed in a shootout after the Maurice bank robbery.
FBI Charged Earl Clayton Randolph as an accomplice.

The Bank of Abbeville and Trust did not waiver after the hold up. Claude J. Broussard was hired as the teller and Dr. Villien returned to manage the bank until his death in 1958. Dr. Villien's son, Joseph A. Villien, Jr., went to work in 1956 as assistant manager of the bank.

Fig. 6.3
Empty vault and trail of blood.

Fig. 6.4
Fatal weapon used by Holdcraft in Bank of Abbeville holdup.

Mercantile Icons Closed

At the outset, the Broussard-Picard Store was a solid contributor to local economy. Brother-in-laws in partnership, Jean "Tee" Camille and Adonis Picard, provided for two large families. The business managed to stay alive after the Great Depression and the families tirelessly continued to diversify inventories and market new items in order to make ends meet. Following Camille's death in 1938, the business began to wane to a point that his wife Ada, and brother-in-law, Adonis, closed the store for good.

Fig. 6.5 *Broussard-Picard Store. From (L-R) Jean Camille Broussard and Adonis Picard, owners, Emedia Hebert, Heloise Picard, Bella Trahan. Note: at the time of this photo, electric lights had not been installed.*

Fig. 6.6 *Broussard – Picard Family Members, ca . 1937*
(L-R) Walter <u>*sitting*</u>*, Lastie* <u>*white shoes*</u>*, Gladys* <u>*holding post*</u>*, Lucille Baudoin Picard,*
Jimmy Picard <u>*sitting*</u>*, Edward* <u>*standing*</u>*, Ada* <u>*right of Ed*</u>*, Heloise "Poop" Picard, Willie*
<u>*child standing*</u>*, Margaret* <u>*sitting top step*</u>*, George "Sumie"* <u>*bottom step*</u>*, Doris* <u>*sitting-legs*</u>
<u>*crossed*</u>*, Leonie "NeNe", Adonis Picard, Thelma* <u>*holding post*</u>*, Annie* <u>*holding post*</u>*, Paul*
Picard <u>*squatting*</u>*, Beb* <u>*holding*</u> *Marilyn* <u>*sitting*</u>*, Alice* <u>*squatting behind Marilyn*</u>*, Wallace*
sitting, Albert Picard <u>*sitting*</u>*, Lona* <u>*behind Wallace*</u>*, and Helen* <u>*behind Albert.*</u>

Broussard-Picard Store was the first business of significant size to close the books in Maurice. But it would not be the last mercantile to go out of business. Residents witnessed Villien Brothers closed its doors in 1968, after one hundred years of continuous business. The modest mercantile was an iconic symbol of local business and trade. The general merchandise store was more than just a source for necessities and household goods. Many employees, throughout the century used their employment there as apprenticeship or stepping stone before establishing businesses of their own.

After the Villien family closed the mercantile business in 1968, the building continued in use for an additional forty years. Local tenants, the Maurice Flea Market and Ray's Appliance, maintained and prolonged the life of the building. With the changing times, the Bank of Abbeville and Trust, a long-time neighbor of Villien Brothers and Company, purchased the site as a part of their long range plan for expansion. The bank had the old building demolished and in 2011 began construction of a new and larger bank building.

Fig. 6.7 *The Abbeville Bank and Trust continues to grow. Villien Brothers and the original Bank of Maurice buildings buckled by bulldozers and backhoes when the Bank of Abbeville broke ground for new buildings on two separate occasions.*

Fig. 6.8 *Villien Brothers General Merchandise Store. (L-R) Albert Villien, Bernice Richard, sister of Savy Duhon; Jeanne Vincent, behind washer, store clerk and postal clerk; Ducre Broussard, leather jacket, store clerk; Ernest Trahan, sweater; John LeBlanc, far right; and three faces not identified.*

62

Fig. 6.9 *Villien Brothers General Merchandise Store.*

Footprints of businesses were indelibly marked by their advertisements of decades ago. Business owners of the 1960s expressed continual support for their local school and advertised as sponsors in the Maurice High School yearbooks. Familiar and repetitive business names in the school yearbook were that of Maurice Drug Store, Will's I.G. Food and Hardware Store, C.A. LeBlanc General Store, G.B. LeBlanc Store, Trahan's Rice Mill, Como's Lounge, Coon's Service Station, Duhon's Slaughter House, Joseph E. Broussard General Merchandise, Villien Brothers and Company, Betty's Cut & Curl Beauty Shop, Scott's Bit Service, Maurice Garage, Vermilion Drum Service, Trahan's Barber Shop and Fidney Trahan's Service Station. All have since closed their doors.

Fig. 6.10 *C. A. LeBlanc General Merchandise Store,* *Corbette A. LeBlanc, Owner. (L-R) Unidentified, Cecile Broussard LeBlanc, Corbette A. LeBlanc, Rachel Martin Villien, Helen Vincent.*

Fig. 6.11 Dixie Auto Lec Store, Ducré Broussard, owner.

Fig. 6.12 Gabriel LeBlanc General Store, Gabriel LeBlanc, owner.

The Broussard Brothers

The Broussard brothers of Maurice are descendents of one of the early families. Fred, Will, Raymond and Roderick learned much of their business skills by working for their father, Ducré Broussard. Ducré and Olive Broussard owned the Dixie Auto-Lec store. After Ducré died in 1951, Fred continued to run his father's business. Raymond, Rod and Will went into partnership with Fred to form Broussard Brothers, Incorporated. In 1966 the business was moved into a new building on East Lafayette Street. In the same year the brother's corporation dissolved and Will continued the business as Will's I.G. and Hardware. Fred, Rod and Ray went on to open their own businesses.

Ricky LeBlanc purchased the business in 2001. He kept the same business name and turned healthy profits for eight years before closing the doors in 2009. The building was reopened in 2011 as NuNu's Supermarket.

Fig. 6.13 *Will's I.G. Food & Hardware, Will Broussard, Owner.*

Fig. 6.14 *Will's I.G. Food & Hardware, Ricky LeBlanc, Owner.*

Fred Broussard opened a new business named Fred's Plumbing and Electric. His shop was in the old Gabriel LeBlanc Store with partners Raymond Broussard and Douglas Trahan. He later moved the business to James Street. In 1995 the business was purchased by his daughter Cathy and son-in-law Carl Villien

In 1968 Raymond Broussard opened Ray's Appliance in the old Villien Brothers store. Raymond leased that building for eighteen years before moving to another location. In 1992 Ray's moved to its present location, which was the former Western Auto store. His brother, Rod operated Rod's TV and Appliance Repair in a shop near his home.

A Surge of Businesses

The nineteen seventies were growing years for Maurice. Though village population was slow to increase, there was a noticeable surge in the number of small business ventures. Many of the following small enterprises may be remembered as a sign of the times when the village was experiencing a glimmer of prosperity. By the end of the seventies, Maurice witnessed a number of establishments disappear from view. Businesses such as Duhon's Welding Shop, Dewey Clark's Grocery, Elizabeth's School of Dance, Global Divers and Contractors, Lavy Duhon's Merchandise, P & S Auto Parts, Touchet Independent Oil Co., Southern Engine & Compressors Specialty, Inc., Herbert Guidry Painting Contractor, Woodley Trahan's Barber Shop and Widley Hebert's Water Well Service had all faded away.

The Outskirts of Town

Businesses located on the outskirts of Maurice were very much a part of the Maurice community. Bert's Exxon, Dale Broussard's Exxon, Duhon's Slaughter House and Giles Trahan Grocery were a few of the Maurice family of businesses.

Fig. 6.15 Giles Trahan Grocery Store, *The store is shown here in an aerial view taken in the late 1950's. At that time Indian Bayou Road (La. Hwy. 92) was a gravel surface and did not become asphalt until the early 1960's.*

Fig. 6.16 Giles and Aglae Trahan owned a farm and grocery one mile west of Maurice on Indian Bayou Road (La. Highway 92).

Recreation and Entertainment

Recreation and entertainment attractions have long been at the core of the community. Whether it was summertime Little League Baseball, an afternoon at a local bush-track, a City Bar Bourré (Booray) game or an evening of listening and dancing to a Cajun-Country band. *La joie de vivre*, was alive and well and in so many ways, kept local economy complete.

From the town's very beginnings some form of entertainment was not far away. Dancing was always a favorite form of entertainment in Cajun country. Before night clubs in Maurice, there was the occasional single fiddler or accordion player who entertained on a local's front porch or at a church or school bazaar. Prior to 1927 there was a pool hall or two that had come and gone, but the night clubs that most people remember are the City Bar, Comeaux's (Como's) Bar (Doug's Main Street Bar), New Wonder Bar, and Hidden Village Bar. Other night clubs such as Clim's in Abbeville or the Blue Room in Milton were only a stone's throw from Maurice.

Area musicians were popular attractions and provided live entertainment on Friday and Saturday nights. Cajun Country Bands like The Friendly Five, Larry Brasseaux or Joey and The Drifters, Junior and the Playboys, and River Road Country Band played at local clubs throughout the region. Joe Hebert, "Joey Bare," was lead singer for his band Joey and The Drifters and recalled having good times at many clubs in the area. His most memorable events were benefits for the Maurice Fire Department and Woodmen of the World in Maurice. The Drifters band members were Wayne Boudreaux on steel guitar, Floyd Menard was bass man, Keno Hebert on drums and Glenn Himel on piano. Rex Champagne also played on drums. George "Buzzy" Villien wrote several songs for Joe's record label "Joey Bare." Songs written by Buzzy were: *Cajun Country Cowboy, I Heard A Rumor,* and *Tomorrow I Won't Be There*. Joe was born in Judice but felt like he was part of the Maurice family. He recalled, "We had a good band and played for all the good night clubs in the area. A couple of our biggest competitors were Larry Brasseux's band and Howard Champagne and the Dukes."

Keno Hebert formed his own country western band after playing with his dad Joe Hebert for many years. Keno's band was called River Road Country Band and has entertained at area clubs since the late nineteen eighties. Keno owns South-End Country Mart grocery which was once Clyves Grocery.

A contemporary and popular entertainer from Maurice is Widley Hebert, Jr., "Junior Hebert" of Junior and the Playboys and a co-owner of the nationally known Hebert Specialty Meats. If one enjoys the flavor of Hebert specialty foods, they will surely enjoy an afternoon of listening to Junior Hebert's Cajun country music.

Fig. 6.17 Recordings by Joe Hebert "Joey Bare", George "Buzzy" Villien wrote several songs for Joe's record label "Joey Bare." Songs written by Buzzy were: Cajun Country Cowboy, I Heard A Rumor, and Tomorrow I Won't Be There. Joe was born in Judice but felt like he was part of the Maurice family.

The first movie house permit was granted in October 1945, when a Mr. Buttergig was given approval by the Board of Aldermen to operate a moving picture as a theater in Maurice without a license. It was common at that time for traveling moving picture shows to operate from temporary quarters such as a large tent. The first theater was located in Hilaire Broussard's old store. The business was operated by Theodore Roger of Lafayette and called the Roger Theater. Roderick Broussard worked at the theater and operated the projector. The second theater was located in the old Albert Picard Furniture Store located on the southeast corner of Joseph Street and Maurice Avenue. The movie house was called the Jan Theater and was operated by Lester J. Gauthier, Sr.

*Fig. 6.18 Maurice **Little League** Team, ca. 1970. Front Row (L-R) Tim Broussard, Timmy Denais, Lynn Broussard, Mark Montet, David Villien, Allen Broussard & Darrel Simon. Back Row (L-R) Coach Fred Broussard, Curt Montet, Danny Broussard, Bennett Comeaux, Gerald Dartez, Ricky Clark, Pete Mathers, Tommy Trahan & Coach Loland Simon. BOW (Boys of Woodmen) Sponsored by Woodmen of the World.*

*Fig. 6.19 Maurice **Babe Ruth** Team, ca. 1969. Front Row (L-R) Karl Abshire, Kim Broussard, Neal Pommier, Dwight Giraurd, Eric Trahan, Pat Abshire, Craig Broussard; Back Row (L-R) Coach Woodley Hebert, Sans Broussard, Pat Broussard, Billy Hebert, Larry Simon, Mike Lalande, Danny Broussard, Aaron Hebert, Lester J. Gauthier, Sr. and Coach Bob Trahan.*

A Village Foundation

Fig. 7.1 *St. Alphonsus Catholic Church, constructed in 1918. This was the third of four structures to serve as St. Alphonsus.*

A Village Foundation
7

St. Alphonsus Church

St. Alphonsus Church history goes back to the early days when residents of Mauriceville lived great distances away from the nearest church. It was an arduous task to attend Mass on Sunday by horse and buggy over the poorly maintained and deeply rutted roads. French and Acadian Catholics took their religion very seriously and Maurice Villien was no exception. He frequently invited a priest from Abbeville to say mass at his home. From St. Mary Magdalen, Fr. T.L. Lamy visited distant areas as far as the Sabine River to say mass. Lake Charles was a mission of Abbeville. Fr. Lamy and successive priests would say Mass in homes of residents on periodic visits to the rural outlying areas. By 1880, Sunday services were held in a private school house on Maurice Villien's property until a church building was built.

In 1886 Maurice Villien built a church on his land near the extreme northeast corner of Section Eleven. The site was along the dirt road and section boundary, south of the section corner at the crossroads now known as Maurice Avenue and Lafayette Street. Construction of the church, even without a permanent assigned clergyman, was in part, fulfillment of his long–range plan to build a small city. In 1889, the existing church building, a rectory and a ten acre parcel was donated by Mr. Villien to the Archbishop of New Orleans. The church was called by area residents, La Chapelle à Maurice. The physical presence of a church became another cornerstone to the village, and in effect the church became *a village foundation.*

Fig. 7.2 La Chapelle à Maurice (L'Eglise de St. Alphonse à Mauriceville) was the first church building of St. Alphonsus. The church was built in 1886 and donated by Jean-Maurice Villien to Archbishop Perché, Dioceses of New Orleans in 1889.

The original act of donation was recorded at the Vermilion Parish Clerk of Court Office. The donation was conveyed on May 28, 1889 from Maurice Villien to Rev. Francis Janssens, Archbishop of New Orleans:

...One certain tract or parcel of land, situated in the parish of Vermilion and lying in the North eastern portion of the North East Quarter of Section Eleven, Township Eleven South of Range Three East, measuring Ten chains, square and containing Ten Superficial Acres. (Note: 1 chain=66 feet). The tract herein described lying and contiguous to the public road on the east and its northern limits being distanced four chains from the Northern line of said quarter section."

"Also one building situated thereon.
The donor, Maurice Villien, further declared that in case it should become necessary to build a church elsewhere in the neighborhood, then in that case this act of donation was to be null and void. The donor further agreed and stipulated that the land therein donated or any portion thereof shall not be signed and sold under any circumstances whatever, and further, should the burial ground or cemetery be located on the tract therein donated, the said Donor reserved to himself and family a plot of ground ten feet square on said tract."

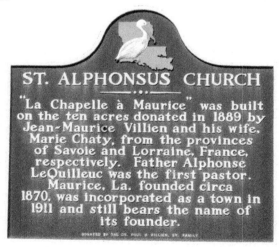

Fig. 7.3 *St. Alphonsus Church, official Louisiana State Historical Marker commemorating construction of the first church in 1889 donated by Jean-Maurice Villien and his wife Marie Chaty.*

> *Jean-Maurice Villien, Jr. and Elina Suir were the twenty-first couple married in St. Alphonsus Church on. Fr. Ferdinand Grimaud officiated the ceremony on October 30, 1893.*

Following his donation, Maurice continued negotiations with the Archbishop of New Orleans to secure a permanent pastor for the church in Maurice. Archbishop Perché was finally instrumental in securing l'Abbe Alphonse LeQuilleuc as the first Pastor of St. Alphonse Parish. The first celebrated Mass in St. Alphonsus was on January 15, 1893. Fr. LeQuilleuc dedicated the Mass to St. Alphonsus de Liguori. After Fr. LeQuilleuc arrived, the name of the church was called L'Eglise de St. Alphonse à Mauriceville. It is presumed that the church took its name from Father Alphonse LeQuilleuc who was named after St. Alphonsus Mary de Liguori, a famous bishop.

Under the direction of New Orleans Diocese, Rev. Francis Janssens coordinated with Fr. Mehault of Abbeville and Fr. S.E. Forge of Lafayette to divide a portion of each of their parishes in 1893 to form a new parish, St. Alphonsus. Fr. Ferdinand Grimaud completed construction of the rectory and established the cemetery in November 1893.

Father Alphonse LeQuilleuc described the limits of St. Alphonsus Parish in church records of June 6, 1893:
"From Abbeville side he listed for the boundaries: Adolph Duhon, Jules Dartez, August Vincent, Lastie Hebert, Severine Hebert, Nunia Hebert, Mozard LeBlanc, John Abshire, Victor Landry, Brunot Broussard and Ursin Broussard. In the direction of Coulee des Cannes to the plateau in front of Madam Paul Rouxel to the road at Amedee Boudreau. From the Lafayette side the channel of Desire Montet and continuing to the extremes of the west (Bayou-Que-Tortue) to Bayou Vermilion and a line straight to Paul Duhon, this is the new parish."

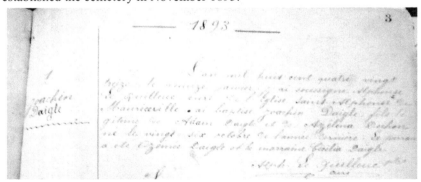

Fig. 7.4 *First Baptism record of L'Eglise de St. Alphonse à Mauriceville,   Joachin Daigle, daughter of Adam Daigle and Azelina Duhon, was the first baptism of 1893. Fr. Alphonse LeQuilleuc performed the baptismal ceremony. Matilde Dora Broussard, daughter of Albert Broussard and Cecile Broussard was the first child baptized.*

In the annual report to the diocese in 1897, Fr. Grimaud listed a church population of 1,400 and 1,200 people received communion. Father Grimaud served in Maurice until 1899 and was then transferred to Carencro, Louisiana. By 1899, Father Augustus Michel Rochard came to the diocese and became pastor at St. Alphonsus. Father Rochard was the parrain (godfather) to Albert A. Villien.

In 1902 it was decided to construct a new church in place of the deteriorating building constructed in 1886. By 1906 the new church was completed and the church population had grown to approximately 3,000. A portion of that population consisted of the local Black population. St. Joseph Parish in Maurice had not yet been established, and the colored people worshipped at St. Alphonsus, the only church in Maurice at that time. The nearest Catholic Church serving colored people exclusively was at the Duson church.

Fig. 7.5
Giles Trahan and Aglae Clark were among the last baptisms in the church built by Jean-Maurice Villien.

Fig. 7.6 Second Church built in 1906

Father W. J. Heffernan served from August 30, 1908 to September 23, 1908. In that year St. Joseph's Society was formed with 112 members. Father Antoine Quenouillere served from September 1908 to December 1908.

The sixth pastor, a native of L'Puy in Auvergne Province, France, was Reverend Celestin Marius Chambon. On Tuesday, September 21, 1909, Father Chambon wrote, in French, a letter to Archbishop J. H. Blenk, a Marist, telling him he had bad news! "Last night a hurricane badly damaged my church and the other buildings of the corporation". Father Chambon was absent from April to July 1910. Reverend Desire Serrazin took over as pastor. Already ordained, Father Serrazin, who had come from France, served several churches in the area, he then retired in France in 1930.

73

In the year the village was incorporated, St. Alphonsus records revealed there were seventy-five white children and forty-two black children that received first communion.

Reverend Louis Laroche came to the diocese from France in 1901 and was assigned to St. Alphonsus on September 10, 1910. By 1915, Fr. Laroche was working at replacing the church which had been damaged by storms and repaired numerous times. The church that was built in 1906 was no longer suitable for use. But, in 1916, another hurricane caused significant damage to the church which expedited start of construction for a new church. The Church Hall was used as the temporary church while construction was underway for the new church.

Fig. 7.7 St. Alphonsus Church Hall was built in 1909.

By 1917 St. Alphonsus population was estimated at 3,500, a stark contrast to the village population of only 328. These figures were an indication that St. Alphonsus was growing significantly. In that year there were eight marriages, 495 children confirmed, 29 burials and 2 adults baptized. Additionally, there were 166 children baptized at St. Alphonsus.

By May of 1918, during the feast of Easter, the third St. Alphonsus Church was completed. The building was fashioned with modern acetylene gas lamps produced by compressed gas piped into the building. A large part of the materials for the construction of the church was furnished by P. U. Broussard of Abbeville. The work of the carpenters was under the direction of J. B. Mouton of Lafayette, and the masonry (pillars and bases of concrete) was done by the assistants of J. B. Gucherau of Lafayette.

Fig. 7.8
The third St. Alphonsus Church was built in 1918. Depicted here are the original windows which were later replaced during renovations in the 1950's.

74

Fig. 7.9 *This photograph, taken ca. 1962, depicts a contemporary style of the third church building following renovations.*

The original architectural style of the 1918 structure consisted of the Romanesque window design with a semi-circular stain glass arch over each aisle window. The original design also entailed a semi-circular window over the front entrance. This building had a transept which did not exist on the two previous church buildings. The openings in the bell tower were unobstructed and the church bell was visible. The building underwent significant renovations in the 1950s under the direction of Father Veekmans. Changes to the building included eliminating the semi-circular arches over the aisle windows and above the main entrance. The openings to the bell tower were enclosed with louvers.

Parishioners purchased a bell for the new church building in January 1920. Father Laroche named Cyprien D. Trahan as parrain (godfather) and Mrs. Jean Villien (Aminthe C. Broussard Villien) as marrain (godmother) of the bell.

Inscription on the face of the bell:
> *"Je m'apple Louise En branle je suis mise Pour que priere on dise Ensemble dans l'eglise"*
> "I am called Louise In ringing I am placed for praying we say together in the church"

Inscription on the opposite side of the bell:
> *"Votre amis je'serai Chretiens des 1e berceau Pour vous je sonnerai Jusqui a votre tombeau".*
> "Your friend I will be Christians from the cradle for you I will ring until your death"

75

Father Laroche was followed by Reverend Francis A. Buquet, a native of France. He was the eighth pastor of St. Alphonsus and served from 1924 to 1926. Father Francis Gerboud "Jabeaux", another native of France, served after Father Buquet and left in 1927. During that time it was customary, as a means of financial support, parishioners purchased or rented church pews.

In November 1927 Father Pierre Marie Gruel, a native of France, became pastor and served until he retired in 1945. Father Gruel was very active in civil affairs and participated at a conference in Baton Rouge in June 1932 concerning a petition to pave the

Fig. 7.10 Father Louis Laroche, Photograph taken ca. 1916-1920.

Maurice Highway. Dr. J. A. Villien, Dr. Carroll J. Mouton, Cyprien D. Trahan and Father P.M. Gruel met with Governor O.K. Allen on matters relating to the six mile unpaved gap between Maurice and Abbeville.

*Fig. 7.11
1921 Map of St. Alphonsus Church, Rectory and Church Hall.*

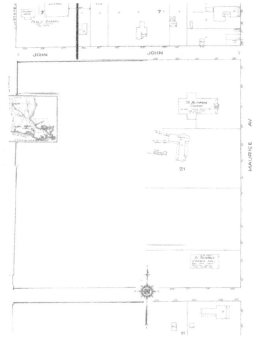

*Fig. 7.12
Godmother "Marrain" of the Bell Aminthe Comeaux Broussard Villien*

Fig. 7.13 *Third Church built in 1918, featured here with a new Church Hall. The priest's Rectory is shown on the left. The Church Hall, in right side of the photograph, was built in 1951 concurrent to other major renovations of the church. The 1951 Church Hall was significantly smaller than the Church Hall built in 1909. (Photograph taken ca. 1950 - 1960)*

Father Albert Bacque, son of Mr. and Mrs. Henry Bacque, was the first priest from the parish. Though he did not serve as pastor in Maurice, he was ordained June 10, 1933 and said his first Mass at St. Alphonsus.

In 1942 Father Gruel compiled a list of men and women of St. Alphonsus who served in the Armed Forces. The Honor Rolls were permanently placed on display in the town hall. The list included seven Black men, three women, two WAACs, Jeanne Dartez and Ruby Duhon and one nurse, Goldie Dupuey.

Father Clifford Gaudin served from May 15, 1945 to March 3, 1946 at St. Alphonsus. Then Father Gommer Eugene Joseph Maurice Veekmans was assigned as pastor. Father Veekmans was an artist and collector of oil paintings and converted one room into an art studio in the rectory. Father Veekmans was instrumental in remodeling the church and did much of the artwork himself.

In 1951 a new Church Hall was built and replaced the 1909 Church Hall. Also in that year, one of Maurice's own, Warren Trahan, was ordained a Benedictine monk at St. Joseph Abbey on May 24, 1951.

Reverend Louis Joseph Napoleon Bertrand, a native of Quebec, Canada, became rector on March 3, 1954. In 1955 Father Bertrand authorized the purchase of an electric bell system for the church.

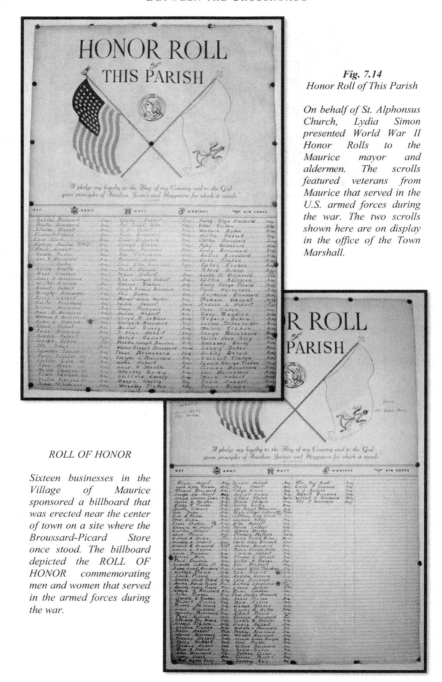

Fig. 7.14
Honor Roll of This Parish

On behalf of St. Alphonsus Church, Lydia Simon presented World War II Honor Rolls to the Maurice mayor and aldermen. The scrolls featured veterans from Maurice that served in the U.S. armed forces during the war. The two scrolls shown here are on display in the office of the Town Marshall.

ROLL OF HONOR

Sixteen businesses in the Village of Maurice sponsored a billboard that was erected near the center of town on a site where the Broussard-Picard Store once stood. The billboard depicted the ROLL OF HONOR commemorating men and women that served in the armed forces during the war.

Father George Howard Simon, was the third native priest of Maurice and was ordained June 8, 1957. His first Mass in St. Alphonsus was on the next day.

In 1966 Father Bertrand started the initiative to build a new church because the existing structure was beyond repair. Father Bertrand died in June 1967 and was buried in the mausoleum at St. Alphonsus.

Father Joseph Robert Dubuc, a native of Quebec, Canada was assigned as pastor at St. Alphonsus in June 1967. The fourth church building began construction in 1968 and finished in 1969. The first Mass was said in the new building on July 26, 1969.

Fig. 7.15
Aerial view of St. Alphonsus Church site, 1970

Monsignor Robert C. Landry, a native of Abbeville, became pastor on May 1, 1974. Father Landry, son of Mr. and Mrs. Robert Landry, was ordained May 28, 1959. He served St. Alphonsus for fourteen years.

In 1974 the first Parish Council was formed and the first bulletin was published. Members of that council in 1974 were H. Fred Broussard, Larry Broussard, Wallace Broussard, Will Broussard, Paul Landry, Robert "Bob" Trahan, Delores Trahan and Alberta V. Winch. Trustees were Lydea Simon and Loubert Trahan. Fred Broussard was appointed trustee a year later upon Mr. Simon's moving to Lafayette.

Fig. 7.16   A view of St. Alphonsus Church bell which was dedicated in 1920.

Fig. 7.17   St. Alphonsus Church and Rectory, ca. 1978.

Patrick Dwayne Primeaux, SM. was the fourth native priest of Maurice. He was born in Abbeville in 1947 and is the son of Mrs. Jeanne Picard Primeaux and the late Isaac Primeaux, former residents of Maurice. Father Primeaux was ordained in 1977.

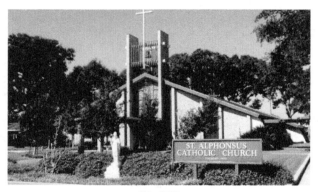

Fig. 7.18
Fourth St. Alphonsus Church and Rectory built in 1969.

Through the leadership of Stanley S. Hebert, Sr., Knights of Columbus Seat of Wisdom Council 8770 was formed in 1984. He was the first Grand Knight of the Council with a charter of 36 members. In honor of his service following his death in 1991, the Council changed its name in 1992 to "Knights of Columbus Stanley S. Hebert, Sr. Council No. 8770."

Reverend Martin Leonards was appointed pastor in August 1988. Fr. Leonards was a native of Rayne, Louisiana. In July of 2002, he was transferred to Duson. Father O. Joseph Breaux, Pastor, at St. Theresa's in Duson, was transferred to St. Alphonsus. Father Breaux is a native of Opelousas, Louisiana and was ordained in 1968.

In 2010 St. Alphonsus Church had approximately 4500 parishioners and 1200 families under pastoral leadership of Father O. Joseph Breaux.

St. Joseph Church

St. Joseph Church became the second Catholic Church in Maurice. The Roman Catholic religion is the oldest in Louisiana and certainly the dominant faith in Maurice. Blacks that were raised Catholic in small communities typically did not have a church of their own. They were usually allowed to attend the local Catholic Church for whites and occasionally were provided pews at the rear of the church. A Catholic church for the blacks was non-existent in Maurice and these were the conditions of the time for blacks prior to 1947.

Before September 1947 black residents of Maurice attended St. Alphonsus Catholic Church or St. Benedict the Moor Church, in Duson, Louisiana. St. Benedict was the nearest church used exclusively by colored people. Bishop Jules B. Jeanmard of Lafayette had authorized the administrators at St. Benedict and parishioners in the town of Maurice to find a parcel of land at Maurice so that the bishop may establish a church there. The black community wanted a church of their own.

In a special meeting convened by a board of directors on August 18, 1946, under jurisdiction of St. Benedict the Moor, Father Francis Wade, SVD, Louis Anderson, Jr. and Frank Morrison met for the first time and officially authorized, by resolution of the board, the purchase of a place of worship for a new church parish.

Fig. 7.19
St. Joseph Catholic Church built in 1947.

Father Francis Wade, SVD, negotiated with Dorice [sic] "Doone" Catalon of Maurice the purchase of the present site of St. Joseph Catholic Church. The site measured 189 feet by 394 feet and was purchased for one thousand dollars.

81

Reverend Francis Wade was one of the first four African-American priests ordained in modern times. Fr. Wade was assigned as pastor and immediately purchased a former U.S. Army Chapel and moved it from Camp Claiborne in Alexandria, Louisiana. While the St. Joseph Church building was under construction, St. Alphonsus Church Parish Hall was used for Sunday masses and St. Alphonsus Church for funerals, weddings and baptisms. On September 7, 1947, Mass was celebrated for the first time at St. Joseph Church.

St. Joseph Catholic Church became a separate parish for the black residents of Maurice in June 1948. Reverend Francis Wade was one of the first four African-American priests in the area.

In 1949 Father Wade initiated construction of a new rectory which stands today. The corporation of St. Joseph Catholic Church was formed on July 28, 1949. The first Stations of the Cross were donated by St. Alphonsus to St. Joseph Church in 1951.

The second pastor was Fr. Leander Martin, SVD (1954 –1955), and following him was Fr. Leo Weng, SVD (1955 – 1966). Fr. Weng was the longest serving pastor in the Church's history. Father Weng was responsible for construction of the parish hall in 1958 and personally painted and maintained the buildings.

Bishop Jules B. Jeanmard invited the first black priests ordained by the Divine Word Missionaries. The first four were Fathers Anthony Bourges, Maurice Rousseve, Francis Wade and Vincent Smith. Two of the four became pastors at St. Joseph in Maurice. Bishop Jeanmard recognized a need and established several separate church parishes for blacks in the diocese. Mother Katherine Drexel, founder of the Sisters of the Blessed Sacrament from Lafayette, also provided financial assistance for black churches in the area and in particular for CCD classes and instruction inside the homes of nearby parishioners.

All of the pastors brought unique qualities with their duties to St. Joseph Church. Father Rousseve arrived at St. Joseph in 1966 and was remembered for visiting and photographing many families in the parish. Father Wenski intrigued his followers with stories about World War II and Father Schuler encouraged traditional African-American worship and use of the current hymnals. Father Heskamp was responsible for expansion of the church hall. Father Richard Zawadzki, SVD was credited in 2005 for construction of the garage and storage building. In August 2005, Father Arochiam began his first pastorate at St. Joseph after serving as associate pastor at Notre Dame Church in St. Martinville.

Annual fund raisers such as bazaars, bingos and gumbo dinners provided necessary finances that sustained the numerous organizations at St. Joseph. The Society of the Divine Word and the Extension Society have also been major contributors in maintaining the church buildings. Through their support organizations such as the CCD Program, the adult and youth choir, the Altar Ladies, the Pastoral Council, Worship Committee and Ladies of St. Peter Claver could not have continued to function. In 2010 there were approximately three hundred families at St. Joseph Church under pastoral leadership of Father Michael Sucharski.

Fig. 7.20 *Amana Christian Fellowship Church*

Amana Christian Fellowship
Amana Christian Fellowship was the first non-denominational church founded in Maurice. It was established in the year two thousand and during the first four years the congregation met at the Maurice Woodmen of the World Hall on Indian Bayou Road for worship. Worshipers built a new facility at 310 Milton Rd. in the year two thousand four. One of the founders of Amana Fellowship was Terrell K. Reed, the pastor in 2011. The congregation numbered approximately 250 people in January 2011.

A Place Called School

Fig. 8.1 *Maurice School, ca. 1913*

A Place Called School
8

Early Schools in Maurice

Before the first Maurice school of 1899, there were several schools in Broussard Cove (Ward Four). Schools were first located on properties owned by Lazard Broussard and David Meaux beginning in 1877. By 1878, a school was built east of Maurice on property owned by Jean Treville Broussard, a well known businessman and land owner of Vermilion and Lafayette Parishes.

The first school in Maurice was built in July 1899, on a one acre site donated by Jean-Maurice Villien. The school site was bordered on the north by Lafayette Street, also known as Indian Bayou Road, on the west by State Street, now Chief H. Fred Avenue, and on the south by John Street. The front of the school house faced the church-yard and cemetery south of John Street. Telesmar Delcambre was the first principal of the school.

Fig. 8.2 *Maurice School ca. 1913-1914; Pictured top right, Annette Maude Gaidry, teacher.*

Fire destroyed the school in 1914 when Rene T. Broussard was principal. Another building was constructed to replace the one destroyed by fire. The smaller of the two was designated as the primary school and the larger was designated as the Junior High School. By 1922 the school was added to the state list of Junior High and Elementary Schools. In that year Emile Ventre became principal. The two wood frame buildings were lighted by oil lamps and heated by wood burning pot-bellied stoves. For a brief period, between 1924 and 1925, while I.R. Brumfield was principal, the school lost its status as a Junior High due to the lack of a failed parish-wide school tax.

Fig. 8.3 *Maurice School ca. 1913-1914.*

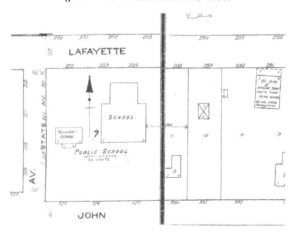

Fig. 8.4 *Map showing Maurice School site in 1921.*
Shown here east of the school is Abraham and Saul Broussard's black smith and wagon shop.

In 1926 the school was moved to the southeast corner of Albert Street and Lafayette Street on property purchased from Mrs. Hilaire Broussard (Corine M. Broussard). The old school house was moved to that location to serve as the elementary building and a new building was constructed to accommodate the high school. During the transition, St. Alphonsus Church Hall became a temporary school house. In 1928, the move from one site to another was remembered as a joyous event and there was a grand march by students from the church grounds to the new school on Albert Street.

Fig. 8.5 1928 Maurice High School Student Body

Fig. 8.6 1928 Girls Basketball Team: front row, Onelia Broussard, daughter of Joseph B.B. Broussard, Elena Hebert, daughter of Lastie Hebert, Alta Picard, daughter of Valerian Picard, Leonie Vincent, daughter of Elie Vincent, Gussie Nugent, daughter of Felix Nugent; (second row) Beulah McDonald, daughter of Ernest McDonald; Noemie Broussard, daughter of Elie Broussard; Edia Duhon, daughter of Numa "Mr. Beck" Duhon; and Edes Clark, daughter of Gladu Clark

Fig. 8.7 1929 Vermilion Parish Boys Basketball Championship Team: front row, Norris Broussard, V.J. Comeaux, John "Ben" Meaux, Robley Duhon, Esson Picard; second row, U.Z. Baumgardner (Principal), Gladu Montet, Dulis Touchet and Leon Broussard and Coach Porter.

87

In 1928 Maurice High was placed on the State High School list and graduated their first classmates. There were only two graduates in 1928, Edes Clark (Edes Clark Broussard) and Beulah McDonald (Beulah McDonald Bell). Edes was the first valedictorian of Maurice High School. U.Z. Baumgardner became principal in 1927 and held that position until 1930.

Fig. 8.8 *Maurice High School students, 1930s*

Leo L. Hebert served as principal in 1934 followed by O.L. Hebert until 1942. During his tenure the Vermilion Parish School Board erected a plaque honoring the dedication of the new Maurice High and Elementary School buildings. The buildings were funded in 1939 by the Federal Public Works Agency, Public Works Administration.

Fig. 8.9 *Maurice High School damaged by storm and flood*

Fig. 8.10 *Maurice High School Class of 1946*

Fig. 8.11 *Elementary School Building, photograph taken ca. 1948*

Fig. 8.12 *High School Building, photograph taken ca. 1948*

Fig 8.13
1932 School Picnic

First row, Alvin Picard, Velma Broussard, Velma Hebert, Lastie Broussard, Tom Baudoin, Lydia Landry, Paul Villien, Ivy Dartez, Ocey Broussard, Billy Broussard, Zula LeBlanc; second row, Emedia Hebert, Edna Mae Creswell, Bertha Vincent, Evelyn Savoy, Rose Amy Broussard, Irene Broussard, Lully Frederick, Hilda Trahan, Viola Meaux, Doris Smiley Edwards (teacher), Oray Huval, Demus Breaux; third row, Esther Baudoin, Edith Winstead; fourth row, Henry Suire, Paul Creswell, Sid Broussard and Paul Duhon.

The canning building was constructed in 1949 and new courses were added to the curriculum. The canning center was dedicated with the latest techniques in vocational-agricultural programs and a workshop. Agriculture and Home Economics became full credit courses in the curriculum.

Disasters of the Forties
Destructive forces of nature were no stranger to this little community in Vermilion Parish. No less than thirty hurricanes visited this region of Louisiana since Jean-Maurice Villien set foot onto the prairie. However, occurrences of tornados were far less frequent than hurricanes. Near midnight on November 7, 1943, a tornado ripped a path of destruction from near Kaplan to north of Maurice. The storm caused considerable damage to area residences, farms, the church and Maurice High School. Killed in the storm were three local residents, Etienne Hebert, his eight-year-old grand-daughter Mary Mae Hebert, and Louis D. Broussard. The high school gymnasium and other buildings received considerable damage, including Principal Romain Picard's home which was lifted and turned around. The school suspended session for more than two weeks afterward.

89

Significant flood events which affected the area as well as Maurice School occurred in 1907, 1927, 1940, 1946, and in March 1947. Though the flood in 1940 was caused by a record rainfall of 37 inches in a ten day period and was considered the most severe to ever inundate Maurice, but to date the 1947 event is remembered by most people. In the memories of present day residents, images of farms and prairies, churches and schools, no place spared, was surrounded by water. Wagons, tractors and boats were the only means of access in or out of town.

Fig. 8.14 Maurice High School (L) and the home (R) of Principal Romain Picard were severely damaged by a tornado in 1943.

A Look at Early Yearbooks

The first Maurice High School yearbook, *Bow Wow*, was published in 1948. The publication marked a new beginning to photographic history of Maurice School. Without yearbooks, faces would have been forgotten. Romain Picard was principal and Hilda Broussard was Editor in Chief of the yearbook staff. The first annual was dedicated to "Miss Annie," Anna Nugent Mouton, a teacher at Maurice School since the late 1920's. That year the high school faculty were listed as Noah Langlinais, Agriculture; Albert Russo, Science; Lona Broussard, Mathematics; Hilda Broussard, Commerce; Lorraine Geyer, English; and Lula Belle M. Bowles, Home Economics.

*Fig. 8.15 First "Bow-Wow"
Yearbook*

*Fig. 8.16 Rachel M. Villien, First Grade
Teacher*

In 1948 Maurice Elementary operated without a second grade teacher. In that year, the elementary teachers were Rachel Villien, first grade; Annie Broussard, third grade; Effie Duhon, fourth grade; Jeanne Primeaux, fifth grade; Martha Melebeck, sixth grade; and Laura Bordeaux, seventh grade.

Since the school's earliest years, Maurice High School students typically excelled in athletics and academics. Students consistently ranked high at Rally Tournaments at SLI in Lafayette and LSU in Baton Rouge. In 1948 thirteen students placed in academic categories while the boys' basketball squad placed second and the track team placed first in most events establishing new regional and state records.

> In 1949, the school's second yearbook was dedicated to Mrs. Rachel Villien for serving 25 years as a first grade teacher. Romain Picard honored Mrs. Villien with the following statement, "Her devotion to her pupils, her cheerful cooperation with the faculty, and her lovable personality have instilled affection and admiration to our hearts... for these and all other reasons which have endeared her to everyone of us, the students and faculty of the Maurice High School extend our appreciation to Mrs. Rachel Villien."

Also in 1949, Randall Stelly joined the faculty as assistant principal and Doris B. Dartez was added as the second grade teacher. Her students remembered her as vivacious, skipping and singing around her classroom. There was no high school graduation that year, one senior, Henry Duhon, graduated with the elementary graduation.

In 1950, the Louisiana state legislature revised the laws requiring all students complete twelve years of education before graduating.

African-American Students

For black students of Maurice and the Broussard Cove area, the first school was located in a small wood-frame private schoolhouse on D.D. Anderson's property located just west of Maurice south of Indian Bayou Road and south of Loubert Trahan's home (present day). The site was part of the original Arvillien Catalon homestead. A public school was later built one mile south of Maurice on the northwest corner of Fuselier Road and La Cote Road. The school was called Southside Maurice Elementary. Black students did not attend school in Maurice until the late 1960s. In 1969 Maurice High School could no longer claim to be an all white school. In that year, Evelyn Thibeaux became the first black student and first black graduate of Maurice High.

From the town's early beginning, African-American students of Maurice attended Vermilion Parish public schools. Many received only basic education and moved away after high school. Most of those who remained here commute to their employment in the larger cities of the area. Only a small number have remained as employees or owners of local businesses.

School in the Fifties

The nineteen-fifties saw the likes of numerous band and music directors. W. Gayre Bazar became Vermilion Parish Music Supervisor, in 1950, and served as occasional music director at Maurice High School. Mr. Bazar later became band director at Kaplan High School. He deeply believed that music contributed to the health of the student and he authored the "Curriculum Guide for Advanced Band" for the Vermilion Parish School Board in 1970.

In 1953, Hermann Fabre became music director, followed by Bobbie Allen in 1955, Raoul Prado in 1957, Paul Chatelain in 1966 and Wilbert Mason in 1972.

The mid-century was marked by the dedication of a new lunch room and hiring of two new high school teachers. Alberta "Berta" Villien who taught English, coached girls basketball and served as Librarian; and Louise Villien who was the Science instructor. Already on-staff were, Lona Broussard, Mathematics, Raymond Ledet, Assistant Principal, eighth grade teacher and basketball coach; Annie Broussard, Commerce; Noah Langlinais, Agriculture; and Lula Belle M. Bowles who taught Home Economics.

Fig. 8.17
Alberta Villien
English Teacher
1950

Fig. 8.18
Louise Villien
Science Teacher
1950

Eradication of the French language on school grounds was required by the Education Act of 1916 and English Education Provision of 1921. It took much longer than expected to expunge the language from the heart, soul and tongues of children who were born speaking the foreign language. Schools were required to implement an English program for all French speaking students. Three decades had passed since state law was enacted forbidding the language in the classroom but still the majority of students in Maurice spoke French in the early 1950s. Cordell Dartez, who later became a principal at Maurice Elementary, remarked, "I started first grade in 1951 and hardly spoke a word of English. We all spoke French at home and didn't have to speak English. We were required to speak English in the classroom." In 1969 The Council for the Development of French in Louisiana (COCOFIL) was created and the French language was introduced into elementary schools.

Fig. 8.19
Band Building built in 1953

Fig. 8.20 *Maurice Junior Band of 1950. Shown here: Watson Simon, Carrol Faulk, Richard McDonald, Clyve Broussard, Beverly Comeaux, Cecil Picard, Katherine Comeaux, George Vincent, Sidney Andrus, Curtis Montte, Curley Broussard, Robert Hebert, Faye Marie Broussard, George Comeaux, Lores Lachaussee, Percy Trahan, Perlis Trahan, Fred Broussard, and Mr. W. Gayre Bazar, Vermilion Parish Music Supervisor.*

Fig. 8.21 *Maurice High School Band 1954 – 1955.*

1967 Majorettes
Connie Fabre, Head Majorette, Beulah Trahan, Janice Gauthier, Melinda Dartez and Rachel Dartez.

Fig. 8.22 *1955 Athletic Court Cecil Picard, Sallie Vincent and John Broussard.*

Fig. 8.23 *1968 Maurice High School Band.*

Romain Picard and Raymond Ledet were Principal and Assistant Principal in 1953 and were supported by thirteen faculty members including, Gabriel Dartez, Agriculture; R.F. Broussard, Science; Hermann Fabre, Band Instructor; Joyce Gauthier, Mathematics; Hilda S. Broussard, Business Education; Yvonne Villien, English; Lula Belle Bowles, Home Economics; Irene Cooper, Sixth Grade; Heloise Neef, Fifth Grade; Rosa Broussard, Fourth Grade; Annie Broussard, Third Grade; Doris Dartez, Second Grade; and Rachel Villien, First Grade. Twelve students graduated from Maurice High in 1953.

The fifties era was also marked by a high level of student participation in numerous school organizations. The Future Business Leaders of America (FBLA) club expanded to a membership of thirty students, 4-H Club had fifty students and nearly as many in the Future Homemakers of America (FHA) and the Future Farmers of America (FFA) organizations. Members of the FFA took first place in Parish Sugar Cane and Rice Festivals. The high school and junior bands also represented the school at fairs and festivals such as the Dairy Festival in Abbeville. The Beginners Band averaged around fourteen members and the advanced band approximately twenty-five members plus four majorettes.

By 1957 some faculty members had moved on to other schools and new faces were added to the teacher's roster. Raoul Prado became the new band instructor; Billie W. Broussard, English; Jeanne Primeaux, Fifth Grade; Edna Landry, Fourth Grade; and R.D. Broussard, Third Grade.

The Sixties

Academically the 1960s was identified by a greater number of students attending annual I.A. and O.A. Rally Tournaments at S.L.I. and State Rally Tournaments at L.S.U. As many as forty students attended tournaments each year. Many participants attended Rally several years in succession and placed in literary events. Since the 1940s the school often ranked first and second in track and field and boys basketball events. Other organizations sent representatives to attend conferences sponsored by Future Business Leaders of America, Future Homemakers of America, and Future Farmers of America.

In 1967, it came of no surprise that nine of the thirteen seniors attended Rally. The high school and elementary school enrollment had not grown significantly through recent years, but entry level first and second grade class enrollments doubled.

In 1968 the Maurice High School Band was awarded "Excellent" at the University of Southwestern Louisiana Band Festival. That year the band also attended the governor's inauguration represented by twenty-eight members and four majorettes. The school was also well represented at the Future Business Leaders Association District Convention at Northside High School in Lafayette with the awards going to Stafford Menard and Virginia Primeaux as "Mr. and Miss FBLA."

The senior class of 1969 consisted of twenty students and proudly graduated the first Black student, Evelyn Thibeaux. Evelyn enrolled here in 1968 and in her senior year attended Rally.

Fig. 8.24 *1973 High School Basketball State Champions.*

Coach Johnny Picard led his basketball team to the Louisiana State Class "C" Championship. The Bulldogs of 1973 were "The Pride of Our Community" winning the state championship twice in five years.

In the same year, the men's track and field team won District, Regional and State Championships. Outstanding members of the championship squad were John Wayne Trahan, Dale Broussard, Rodney Trahan, Stafford Menard, Mark Leach, Tommy Ferguson, Harold Duhon and Roger Viator.

Fig. 8.25 *1973 High School Track and Field Class "C" State Champions*

Front row (L-R) Larry Winters, Eric Trahan, Glynn Broussard, Daniel Broussard, Kim Broussard, Don Comeaux, Virgil Vincent and Keith Sellers; standing, (L-R) Keith Landry, Michael Norman, Kenneth Trahan, Russell Guidry and Russell Sellers.

The Final Decade

Each year the number students continued to increase and as a result by the early seventies additional faculty and staff were hired to meet the growing needs. The seventies would be the final decade of the high school's history. Jules Duhon and Raymond Ledet, Principal and Assistant Principal, were supported by thirty-eight teachers, aides, a secretary and twenty additional support staff such as cooks, bus drivers, janitors and food staff. In1973, the school marked another mile-stone by forming the first boys baseball and first girls baseball squads.

Fig. 8.26 First Boys Baseball Team, 1973

Standing (L-R) Mark Cooper, Eric Trahan, Craig Broussard, Pat Broussard, Dwight Girauard, Keith Sellers, Russell Sellers, Kneeling: Glenn Broussard, Kim Broussard, Don Comeaux, Roger Montet, Danny Broussard Virgil Vincent, Martin Gauthier, Sitting: George Sellers, Brian Broussard, Garrett Broussard, Leon Broussard, Tab Comeaux.

Fig. 8.27 First Girls Baseball Team, 1973

Standing (L-R) Mary Joseph, Vickie Broussard, Cindy Broussard, Marlene Denais, Pearl Trahan, Sandra Picard, Liz Landry, Kathy Picard, Kneeling: Pat Trahan, Melanie Broussard, Tessie Broussard, Mona Montet, Jan Hebert, Darlene Guidry.

In 1975 the boys' baseball team climbed to second in state with a ten win and four loss record. They were coached by Willie Broussard and Johnny Picard. Again in 1977 Maurice High took the honors as District 13-B baseball champions under leadership of Coach Willie Broussard.

The school continued to expand and in 1979 there were forty-three teachers and administrators. That year thirty-nine seniors graduated followed by thirty-two seniors in the final year. The last yearbook issue of *Bow Wow* was dedicated to Mr. Jeffery DeRouen. In May of 1979 Maurice School concluded its final decade as a high school.

Fig. 8.28 The Last Bow Wow yearbook cover, Maurice High School, 1980

High Schools Merged

The new North Vermilion High School was in its first year beginning in September 1980. High school students from Maurice were relocated to the new school several miles south of Maurice, near the community of Leroy. The high school was consolidated with other area schools. Maurice merged with students of Indian Bayou, Leroy and Meaux communities. North Vermilion High School included grades seven through twelve. Maurice High School principal, Jules E. Duhon also transferred to assume the same position at North Vermilion. A resident of Leroy, Jules Duhon was the last principal at Maurice High School and the first at North Vermilion and was very much in favor of the consolidation.

Concurrent to the opening of North Vermilion High School, the old Maurice High School campus was converted to Maurice Elementary (K-6). Under direction of Principal Cordell Dartez, the school embarked on a different educational journey, without the presence of high school students. In less than six months, all dreams and aspirations for the new elementary school was frozen in time. On February 11, 1981, the school, for the second time in its history, was ravaged by fire. The buildings were totally destroyed. Temporary buildings were moved-in to

Fig. 8.29 *Maurice Elementary destroyed by fire.*

On a frigid early morning in February 1981, Maurice Elementary was destroyed by fire. The gymnasium, offices, classrooms, locker rooms and cafeteria were totally destroyed.

house the elementary students until permanent buildings were constructed. The permanent buildings would not be finished until 1986.

In 1981 Maurice students who would have attended Maurice High School were joined with their arch rivals from Meaux High School to attend the new North Vermilion High School. The previous mascot of Maurice, the "Bulldog" was replaced by the "Patriots". The inscription in Volume I of North Vermilion yearbook read: "This year age old rivals Maurice and Meaux were united together we work; Together we play. Work for tomorrow; forget yesterday. Our strength is doubled. Our potential is strong. One year of fun two as one."

Maurice Elementary School

Cordell Dartez was hired as the first principal of the new Maurice Elementary School in 1980. Cordell was a native of Maurice and a 1965 graduate of Maurice High. Cordell married Linda Baumgardner, who also graduated Maurice High (class of 1966), and the only native of Maurice to ever attain valedictorian at the University of Southwestern Louisiana.

Cordell Dartez served as principal from 1980 to 1988. During his tenure in 1986 he was awarded the "Top Louisiana Elementary Administrator" and placed on the national list as a "Top Ten Elementary Administrator". The award was bestowed by Vice President Walter Mondale in a ceremony at the Capital in Washington, D.C. The distinguished award, among other things was based on a performance oriented program for children grades one through six initiated by Cordell. The program, in part, was initiated to assist self esteem of foster kids. There were many foster children enrolled at Maurice Elementary at the time. An example of one of his students that achieved success through this program is Denise Boutté (Denise Winters) who has starred in television episodes such as Boston Legal, Days of Our Lives, and Everybody Hates Chris.

Mascots, in the early years, were adopted by a homeroom class. Some may have had two mascots. In 1948, on the front cover of the first yearbook was a single mascot of Maurice High. The high school mascot remained Bulldog until Maurice merged with Meaux to form North Vermilion High School. North Vermilion's mascot became the Patriots. The *Bulldog* remained the mascot of Maurice Elementary until 1985. The mascot was then changed to *Jr. Patriots*.

Patricia "Pat" Webb graduated from Iota High School and attended McNeese University where she graduated with a Masters in 1976 and received Plus 30 from University of Louisiana at Lafayette in 1982. Pat first served as Guidance Counselor at North Vermilion High School and then Assistant Principal at J. H. Williams Middle School in Abbeville before starting as principal at Maurice Elementary School. She became the second principal at Maurice Elementary in 1988. She served as principal until 2005. Her assignment at Maurice was like a dream that came true. She had loved her association with the students and residents while at North Vermilion and wanted to return to the area. The country quality and charm of the people around Maurice was a characteristic that she loved and cherished. Affectionately describing her students and the people of the town, she coined a phrase that appropriately depicted some folks of the area as "sophisticated country people."

Patricia felt that she was lucky to work with a faculty and staff who were very professional and cared about the students. While there, some of the most outstanding memories came from the organizations such as 4-H and Beta Club. She was extremely proud of the outstanding music program under the direction of Linda Goodman. The program was designed to teach more than just instruments, but included dance, singing, acting and band. The program effectively provided much more, she said, "The most productive element of the program was not the acting and singing, it was the confidence, self-esteem and pride of ownership that students gained from the program. This spilled through to the educational setting of the school...I look back with much pride as I remember my years at Maurice Elementary."

Greg Theriot served as the principal of Cecil Picard Elementary from 2005-2008. Prior to his tenure there, he served as an assistant principal at both Maurice Elementary and North Vermilion High School. He started his teaching and coaching career in Vermilion Parish at Henry High School where he served as the English department head and coached basketball, cross-country, and baseball. In 1990, he was named the LHSBA Class C Coach of the Year after leading his team to the state championship. In 1992, he transferred to North Vermilion High School where he taught English and coached football, girls basketball and baseball. As an assistant coach with Brent Broussard, he again won another baseball state championship in 1994 when the Patriots became Class 2A champions.

He is a native of nearby Milton where his parents owned and operated Theriot's Grocery. He is a 1983 graduate of Comeaux High School and earned a Bachelor of Science degree in Education from USL in 1987 and owns a Master's Degree in Administration and Supervision from McNeese State University in 1999.

In his tenure as principal of Cecil Picard Elementary, he had a number of unique and interesting experiences. During his first school year, he served as the hurricane shelter director after Hurricane Rita and also saw his school platoon with Dozier Elementary. In his second year the school name was changed from Maurice Elementary to Cecil Picard Elementary to honor the late state superintendent, Cecil Picard, who grew up on the grounds of the school. He treasures the time he spent at Maurice and now serves as the principal of North Vermilion High School where he has been named the Vermilion Parish Middle School Principal of the Year.

Wendy Stoute graduated Magna Cum Laude in 1989 from the University of Louisiana at Lafayette. Her desire to become a better educator resulted in attaining several certifications including a Master's Degree Plus 30 and a Specialist Degree in 2003. Her first professional teaching assignment was at Erath Middle School. She subsequently worked as a counselor and assistant principal at J.H. Williams Middle School in Abbeville.

In 2008, she was hired as principal at Cecil Picard Elementary. Her goals were to introduce cutting-edge technology to her school. Wendy was successful in obtaining Promethean interactive whiteboards for the classrooms. This technology is a large display board consisting of the power of a computer that allows students to engage and interact with vivid images, video and audio. Because of this technology, the village school was able to keep pace with other schools and prepare students for the many changes of the future.

Recently, the federal government set a goal for all public elementary schools to reach a "School Performance Score" of one hundred twenty by the year 2014. Wendy established a process to achieve the goal and became the first school in the Parish to attain the score.

Wendy characterized her work in the following manner: "I am reminded on a daily basis why I began my career as an educator so many years ago. Daily, I greet my students in the morning as they enter and again in the afternoons, as they make their way to the bus. Never has a day gone by that a student hasn't thanked me for 'making the school' or that I haven't received a hug, smile or other encouraging words. I am grateful to be a part of their lives, this community, and our school, Cecil Picard Elementary."

Paulette Gaspard began as principal at Cecil Picard Elementary in June 2011. She is a native of Kaplan and the daughter of Paul and Dora Broussard. She is a 1983 graduate of Kaplan High School. Paulette received a Bachelor of Arts degree from University of Southwestern Louisiana and a Master's Degree in Educational Leadership from McNeese State University. Her teaching experience included assignments at Morse, Henry, Kaplan, Rene Rost and Jesse Owns Elementary Schools. She previously served as assistant principal at Cecil Picard Elementary and J. H. Williams Middle School before her current assignment as principal.

Paulette expressed that she is "excited about the opportunity to be involved with a community that supports their elementary school teachers, students, and staff. I plan to continue leading and guiding the teachers of Cecil Picard Elementary in enhancing the students' academic experience".

Principals 1899 – 1938

Telesmar Delcambre	1899
Rene T. Broussard	1914
Emile Ventre	1922
U.Z. Baumgardner	1927
Leo L. Hebert	1934
O.L. Hebert	1938

Fig. 8.30
Romain Picard, Principal
1942 -1966

Fig. 8.31
Cecil Picard, Principal
1966 – 1969

Fig. 8.32
Jules Duhon, Principal
1969 – 1980

Fig. 8.33
Cordell Dartez, Principal
1980 – 1988

Fig. 8.34
Patricia Webb, Principal
1988 – 2005

Fig. 8.35
Greg Theriot, Principal
2005 – 2007

Fig. 8.36
Wendy Stoute, Principal
2007 – 2010

Fig. 8.37
Paulette Gaspard, Principal,
2011 -

101

Growth of Maurice School began with only small wood framed buildings on one acre of land. The student body had less than forty students and only a hand full of teachers who taught multiple grade levels. During the last century the little school underwent numerous changes and transformations. It began as an elementary school and grew into a competitive institution preparing students for college and successful careers.

The evolution of the school has made a full circle and once again serves only elementary students kindergarten through sixth grade. The student enrollment in 2011 breached seven hundred and consisted of more than fifty faculty, staff, helpers and special assistants. The campus today occupies more than eleven acres with seven buildings. The buildings are around twenty-five years old but their interiors are fully up-to-date with modern educational tools and current technology. There is nothing *old school* about today's Cecil Picard Elementary. The band building, the oldest structure standing, was constructed in 1953 and exists in memoriam of years gone-by. Education is the heart and soul of Maurice and its institution is no longer just *a place called school.*

Fig. 8.38 *Cecil Picard Elementary at Maurice*

Businesses of Today

Fig. 9.1 *Bank of Abbeville and Trust. A new branch bank building under construction in 2011-2012 will replace the existing building which was completed in 1970.*

The **Bank of Maurice** was founded in 1921 by Dr. Joseph A. Villien, Sr. The bank was purchased by Abbeville Bank and Trust in 1933. Dr. Villien continued as manager of the Abbeville Bank and Trust Maurice Branch until he retired in 1958. His son, Joseph A. Villien, Jr., went to work at the bank in 1956 and became manager after his father retired. Joseph Villien managed the bank until his death in 2001. Ronald Leger, son-in-law of Joseph A. Villien, Jr., began working at the bank in 1980 and became manager after Joseph Villien died.

103

Businesses of Today
9

Oldest Commercial Buildings Standing

Today when visitors travel south, out of Lafayette, on U.S. Highway 167, they enter Vermilion Parish as they cross over Coulee Ile des Cannes. First, viewers are greeted by a very noticeable sign inscribed *Bienvenue à Vermilion Parish.* The entryway is flanked by greenery and unpretentious structures that are discernibly not of historic significance. A great many of the commercial buildings are less than half century in age. However, one might notice the following as the oldest commercial structures as they travel through Maurice.

Maurice Avenue:
> Shear Indulgence Beauty Salon was once the home of Philomene Rouen Gaidry, mother of Mrs. J.A. Villien. The structure was built around the 1920s and moved to its present location in the 1970s.
>
> Villager's Café was formerly the office of Dr. Harold G. Trahan and now owned by Mary Beth Broussard.
>
> City Bar was established in 1927 and the present structure was built following a fire in 1956 and owned by Mathiew Trahan.
>
> Maurice Garage was built by Albert Villien in 1923.
>
> Pelican Wood Works building was originally built by Corbette A. LeBlanc. C.A. LeBlanc General Merchandise was established in the 1940s.
>
> Gabriel LeBlanc Store was built in the 1950s and the structure is presently vacant.

Chief H. Fred Avenue:
> Delhomme Funeral Home was formerly St. Alphonsus Church Rectory. In 1978, the old rectory building was remodeled and converted to a funeral home.

East Lafayette Street:
> NuNu's Grocery was formerly Will's IG Store and Hardware and built in the 1960s.

John Street:
> Maurice Cotton Gin was built in 1925

Photo Inventory of Businesses

The following pages comprise a photo inventory of businesses in Maurice. Refer to the *Figures* index (*page 153*) in the back of this book for a names directory.

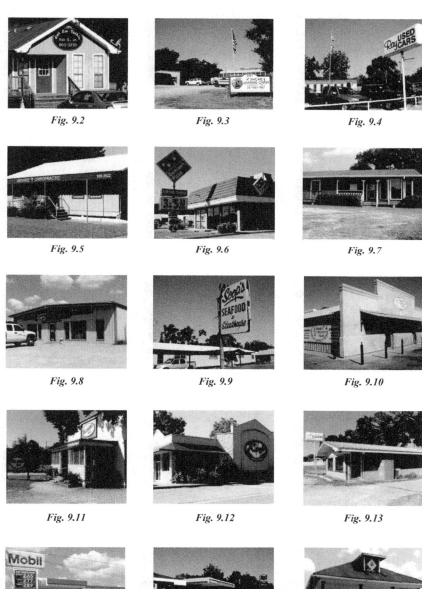

Fig. 9.2   Fig. 9.3   Fig. 9.4

Fig. 9.5   Fig. 9.6   Fig. 9.7

Fig. 9.8   Fig. 9.9   Fig. 9.10

Fig. 9.11   Fig. 9.12   Fig. 9.13

Fig. 9.14   Fig. 9.15   Fig. 9.16

Fig. 9.17

Fig. 9.18

Fig. 9.19

Fig. 9.20

Fig. 9.21

Fig. 9.22

Fig. 9.23

Fig. 9.24

Fig. 9.25

Fig. 9.26

Fig. 9.27

Fig. 9.28

Fig. 9.29

Fig. 9.30

Fig. 9.31

By-passing Maurice

Today a chronicle of businesses in Maurice would be very different had Mayor Corbette LeBlanc succumb to bureaucratic proposals radiating from Baton Rouge in 1975. The Louisiana State Department of Highways was proposing to re-route U.S. Highway 167 away from the center of Maurice. The plan caused a morose mood among business owners who knew that such a plan would have diverted customers away from the village's main thoroughfare and away from their storefronts. Corbette stood-fast and was adamantly opposed to a highway bypass. His view of what would have happened to the town had lawmakers got their way, was very noteworthy and his actions likely affected the course of history here. Mayor LeBlanc convinced officials at the Louisiana State Highway Department and Governor Edwin Edwards to four-lane the existing route through the middle of town and to drop the plans for a bypass. Today, the four-lane commercial corridor is vibrant and lined with an eclectic list of enterprises.

In spite of rapid regional growth during the last half century, Maurice experienced progress in a very traditional way, one business at a time. The independent mom and pop businesses and slow pace of growth may have been the key to survivability, as a village, centered between two cities. Former Mayor Barbara Picard once remarked that "we have to have progress, but we really want to maintain the small town atmosphere as much as possible. That is why people live here". That sentiment has continued to transcend into the present day as the mayor and aldermen are cautious in their review of each new business request.

(Continued from page 106) A photo inventory of today's businesses in Maurice.

Fig. 9.32

Fig. 9.33

Fig. 9.34

Fig. 9.35

Fig. 9.36

Fig. 9.37

Fig. 9.38

Fig. 9.39

Fig. 9.40

Fig. 9.41

Fig. 9.42

Fig. 9.43

Fig. 9.44

Fig. 9.45

Fig. 9.46

Fig. 9.47

Fig. 9.48

Fig. 9.49

Fig. 9.50

Fig. 9.51

Fig. 9.52
The City Bar is world famous and home of the Bourré game. Bourré (Boo-Ray or Booray) is a favored Louisiana trick-taking card game of French origin. It is said the rules of the distinctly unique card game were written here.

The City Bar is still in business today because the main thoroughfare through town was not re-routed. The famous watering hole may have closed its books had a by-pass been constructed.

Spotlight on the 70s and 80s

The 1970s and early 80s were marked by good economic times when Louisiana's oil boom fueled expansion of local economies. In Maurice, many of today's businesses were fledgling establishments that began during this era. Many people remember start-ups like the Street Scene Boutique owned by Mr. & Mrs. Robert Clark and Maison deFleur owned by David and Judy Lalande. In 1972, businessman Widley "Soop" Hebert and his wife, Doris, took a special interest in Maurice and opened a small seafood restaurant, Soop's Seafood and Steak House. The restaurant grew to national popularity along with its companion business, Hebert's Specialty Meats. Soop's three sons, Wayne, Widley Jr. and Sammy, operated the specialty meat shop. It is said that the Hebert family coined the term

Fig. 9.53
Widley "Soop" Hebert
Soop's Restaurant

"Turducken" but there was no doubt that the family business is home to the "Debonded Chicken" and its national popularity contributed to the notoriety of the Village of Maurice.

Maurice was a small dot on the map which became a little larger and illuminated a little brighter when the national spotlight turned toward two personalities who claimed the little village as their home. Kent J. DesOrmeaux raised community pride after winning his first career stakes race in 1986 at the Maryland City Handicap at Laurel Park Race Course.

Kent grew up on a farm near Maurice and lived a different pace of life than most Cajuns. He attributed his affiliation with racing horses to his early years of 4-H Club involvement. He continued to develop his skill as he participated in racing at area quarter horse tracks and then, when he became of age, at Evangeline Downs in Lafayette.

Kent was inducted into the National Museum of Racing Hall of Fame in 2004 as the jockey with the record for the most races won in 1989. Kent also added to his fame after winning his third Kentucky Derby. He acquired an exhaustive list of records in horse racing, breaking national and international records.

Fig. 9.54
Kent J. DesOrmeaux
The record breaking horse racing
jockey of Maurice

Fig. 9.55
Alexander Caldwell
World famous designer
of the modern Fabergé
Egg

Alex Caldwell also brought home pride to Maurice when he initiated production of a modern version of the "Fabergé Egg" in 1987. He and business partner, Vivian Tullos, created a lady's accessory which was a jewelry masterpiece of gemstones and decorations. Their product trade mark became known worldwide as "Vivian Alexander."

In 1984, Mr. Caldwell moved to the outskirts of Maurice on Bayou Vermilion near Milton. The land was pasture land owned by the Picard family for generations. Alex transformed the property from farmland to a small estate home site. One of the early projects was the design and construction of a cypress barn to be used for storage, recreation, and projects. In 1990 the structure was turned into a small hobby turned business venture. Using goose eggs from the plethora of foul on the property, Alex began decorating egg shells as a sideline venture. The business grew into a worldwide enterprise, with his product sold in gift shops in multiple countries. Alex's girlfriend, Vivian, helped to name this new venture Vivian Alexander.

Fig. 9.56 Soop's Restaurant
The Hebert sisters are known for serving the finest of Louisiana's traditional gumbos at Soop's Seafood and Steakhouse Restaurant on Maurice Avenue. A delightful meal is always served with a smile from Sharon Byers.

From the day Soop's Restaurant opened, the **Hebert sisters**, Rachael Hebert "Head Sister", Wanda H. Duhon, Stephanie H. Villien, Yvonne H. Shumaker, Leah H. Mistich, Jennifer H. Jones, Mandy Hebert, Phyllis H. Villien and Sharon H. Byers have prepared original Cajun dishes with traditional family recipes. Secrets to a good dish are about the things that are left out. Celery, bell peppers and wine are not original Cajun cooking. "The simplest is the best", said Rachel in an interview with C. Richard Cotton of the Baton Rouge Advocate newspaper.

Area residents not only love the taste of good food, they know how to cook it. In Maurice, residents understand and appreciate living in the heart of nature's pantry. This region of coastal Louisiana offers almost everything a chef might want. At Mr. Keet's Restaurant, Gerard and Helen Baudoin, stewards of Cajun cuisine, know how to acquire the best of south Louisiana's bounty and capture the basic flavors through Cajun cooking. They incorporate tradition into every dish served. They initially opened a drive-thru "take-out" business serving boiled crawfish. Success soon led the business into a full service restaurant called Mr. Keet's and they have been serving great Cajun dishes since. The history behind the unusual restaurant name originated with Grant, the

Fig. 9.57 *Mr. Keet's Restaurant*
Helen and Gerard Baudoin, owners

owner's four year old son. Little Grant Baudoin could not pronounce the name of Gerard's friend Mr. Keith Ratcliff. His pronunciation only came out as Mr. Keet. When it came time to give the restaurant a formal name, words resonated as a unique title with a Cajun pronunciation.

Will's IG Grocery and Hardware, established by Will Broussard, closed for business in 2009 which left Maurice without a large grocery store for nearly two years. Since closing its doors, residents of Maurice had to travel to nearby communities for groceries. The old store was reopened in 2011 as NuNu's supermarket.

A Four-lane Roadway

Mayor Corbette LeBlanc, assured business owners that they were not going to lose ground because of a bureaucratic plan to by-pass Maurice with a new roadway. He worked to preserve commercial frontage and thought businesses would be ever more visible on a four-lane avenue. The four-lane project on Maurice Avenue was completed in 1975, and Governor Edwin Edwards proudly assisted Mayor LeBlanc in a ribbon cutting ceremony.

Mayor LeBlanc's diligence continued beyond his administration as subsequent mayors Picard and Ferguson worked with city aldermen and U.S. senators and representatives to continue LeBlanc's projects and to secure federal grants for other brick and mortar projects. The grants by the Department of Housing and Urban Development enabled upgrades to the wastewater treatment plant and potable water systems, including a new water tower, which has encouraged opening of new businesses.

Fig. 9.58 A grand celebration and ribbon cutting ceremony commemorating the completion of a four-lane widening project of Maurice Avenue and U.S. Highway 167 between Lafayette and Abbeville in 1975.

Looking Back

Lost and gone are cotton gins, rice mills, black smiths and country stores that once were the fabric and economic foundation here. No longer are there agricultural related businesses that dominate the local economy or the small local family owned farms that once provided economic stability. So many of the old iconic businesses are gone and everyone of those business owners had a story to tell about their past but few people of today will ever hear them.

Today stories of bygone days still echo on the walls of three long standing establishments. The Bank of Abbeville Maurice Branch, Ray's Appliance and the City Bar are among the surviving institutions of Maurice.

Since the earliest days, only a handful of commercial buildings have escaped demolition and despite efforts by a small group of preservationists, soon other old buildings may follow suit by way of the bulldozer.

A casual look from a distance, it appears that the small town has long been ignored by today's fast track society. Small communities of meager populations and a sleepy economy often have become remnant settlements. Many of the historic aspects of the village have simply begun to disappear but not because of sprawling urban waves of large residential and commercial developments stemming from its neighbors of Lafayette and Abbeville. But only by its' own hand, new has replaced the old, a natural evolution of commercial changes. Maurice might not fall under a news headline of *Business is Booming*, rather it is, as Mayor Picard once stated, simply "a progressive little community". Altogether the local economy is led by a whole new list of businesses catering to twenty-first century demands.

Maurice has held its own, and to this day it is recognizable as an independent community and not so much a suburb of the neighboring cities. It is meeting contemporary challenges and perhaps maybe in line to become the next major growth center of Vermilion Parish. In the dawn of its second centennial, Maurice is still growing one enterprise at a time. Recently two new commercial and significantly large projects were completed on the south side of Maurice. The Acadian Apartments, a large seventy-two unit multi-family residential complex, was completed on Maurice Avenue in 2011. And in January 2012, Pelican Pointe Healthcare and Rehabilitation was completed. It is a state-of-the-art one hundred twenty bed long term care facility on Milton Road.

Maurice has been poised for the attention of large retailers and investors in search of new markets for some time. Only that, here, the villagers plan to control their own destiny. Controlled growth is their key to maintaining that "small town character" that most residents desire.

113

Merchants and residents of Maurice have recognized that small communities do not have the problems of bigger cities. The quality of life is abundant here and people want to keep it that way, even if the rate of growth remains the same.

Fig. 9.59
This photo is of Maurice Avenue ca. 1916-1920. Father Louis Laroche is shown standing in the center of Maurice Avenue. Visible behind the wagon wheel are: Villien Brothers, Dr. J.A. Villien's office and drug store and Le Magasin à Maurice.

Fig. 9.60
This photo depicts approximately the same location in 2012 as the photo on the left of Father Louis Laroche. In this photo, the newest Bank of Abbeville is shown on the far left (under construction) and adjacent to the bank building constructed in 1969. Not visible, behind the trees on the right is the home of Michael and Sonia L. Comboy, formerly the home of Corbette A. LeBlanc, Sr., and originally the home of Jean-Maurice Villien, Jr.

A Plan for Tomorrow

Fig. 10.1 *Aerial view of Maurice in 1970*
When surveyors trampled overland to stake out section corner marks, their straight paths along the section lines provided ease of passage in contrast to the old meandering and confusing trails and wagon roads that crisscrossed the prairie. Landowners set fences along the section property lines. This later came to play an important feature when Jean-Maurice Villien began planning a little city. It was a plan typical of prairie towns with a street grid laid out on section lines and situated between the crossroads at section corners.

A Plan for Tomorrow
10

Maurice Villien's original street layout of more than a century ago followed the standard gridded town concept of the nineteenth century. The plan called for small individual lots within walking distance of church, school and businesses. The town was developed in a traditional way, where as lots and blocks were laid out on a grid system which had the same function as the national land survey system. City blocks were planned in varying dimensions, some were three hundred feet square and others were approximately three hundred by four hundred feet. Lot sizes varied but averaged fifty feet in width and depth ranging from one hundred forty to one hundred fifty feet. The lot sizes were basically designed for small bungalow sized homes of the early twentieth century with little room to accommodate the impending larger dwellings of the mid to late twentieth century.

Traditionally city plans include areas or sites designated for key land uses. In Maurice, the first church and the first school yard were pre-determined by the founder. Commercial and residential uses were allowed to build on any other lot without restriction. However, it is puzzling to this day whether there was ever any designated area for the seat of government and services. One might wonder: because the original plan clearly depicted Block 9 at the center of town, why was it absent of interior lots? Was it intended to be the hub of governmental buildings and services? One such public building was the jail. Evidence indicates that it was constructed, but no record of its whereabouts can be found. The answer remains a mystery.

After staking lots and advertising their sale, promoters waited for residents and businesses to come. The optimistic settlement did not see residents pour in as hoped. From the beginning, they came at a pace not more than a trickle. Perhaps the abundance of available land all around Maurice was more attractive than living on closely arranged lots in town.

Little in the way of land planning has been done since the first plan was carved into the earth. During the 1950s, the town's largest land holder, the Villien family, commissioned drawings for a street layout on parcels in the northeast part of town. The plans for Villien Subdivision were only partially implemented. Within the last forty years, there have been only a couple of small residential subdivisions developed within the corporate limits of Maurice. Most of the community's growth, residential and commercial, has occurred along the existing state roads or secondary streets of the town. From the outset, the community as a whole has managed to remain relatively unscathed by erratic construction of mixed land uses. Put simply, the community has functioned remarkably well without the typical subdivision and zoning regulations in place to guide or control land use development.

In the first eighty years, the population of Maurice seemed as though there was a force preventing it from rising above 500 people. In World War II, men and women were scattered around the world but their return home had little effect on the population total. Unlike so many of its contemporary small towns, Maurice's population actually declined in 1950 and did not begin to rise to pre-war levels until the 1960's. Even while there was substantial regional growth, both new development and population growth here were stagnated. It is interesting to note, however, that church and school attendance was disproportionately greater than community population.

Regardless of the population change since the founding fathers signed the Proclamation of 1911, the quality of life changed significantly. Installation of community potable water systems, sewage treatment, electric service, telephone service and paved roads all translated to improved standard of living. Additionally, in the first half of the twentieth century, mass produced and affordable appliances began showing up in homes and automobiles gradually replaced buggies and wagons. The post-war era also brought about natural gas, propane gas and electric appliances into homes. Means of communication swiftly moved from telegraph, radio and newspaper to telephone and television in every home. Homes of the 1960s no longer required domestic production of goods. Rooms designated for home canning of vegetables and fruit, churning butter, pasteurizing milk and spinning yarn were home activities that became *passé*. Most people living in rural communities had transformed from being producers to consumers.

By the 1970s, during the regional oil boom, there was much talk about planning for future needs of Maurice. In early 1979 the Board of Aldermen appointed the first seven-member Planning Commission. The board consisted of the following members: J.C. Meaux, Carroll Comeaux, Ollie J. Chargois, Robert Delhommer, Elodie H. Broussard, Geraldine Chargois and Ethel St. Julien. However, diminished citizen interest and participation led to the board's termination by the early 1980s. The idea of planning for the future was pushed away as a low priority of citizens and civic leaders.

As the technology of the world improved at lightning speed during the latter half of the century, the 1990 population had not advanced as much and continued to remain below 500. Only in recent decades has long range planning come to be part of this community's town hall discussions. Today, while farming activity surrounds the town, the commercial retail and service sector in Maurice represent the dominant employment base. The impetus of commercial activity has generated an interest in long-range planning. The idea of planning and preservation are rapidly gaining more popularity with residents throughout the town than ever before.

In 2009, Bank of Abbeville and Trust purchased the old Villien Brothers store as a part of a planned expansion of the bank. A newly formed non-profit preservation organization called, Maurice Historical Preservation Society, spared the original store and oldest building of the community from demolition. The Bank of Abbeville donated the building and a parcel of land was donated by Dr. Marc J. Villien, great grandson of the village founder, to the preservation group. The Society is presently renovating the structure which was named Le Musée à Maurice. It is through this grassroots effort to preserve history that has moved the community toward planning for the future.

Fig. 10.2 *Le Musée à Maurice and Official Louisiana State Marker*

Recently, in town hall meetings, citizens of the community displayed interest in planning for the twenty-first century. The citizens expressed that change was inevitable but their desire was for the community to maintain its *small town character*. The idea of keeping Maurice small and quaint was fostered during Mayor Picard's era and rekindled when Mayor Ferguson held community meetings to discuss future plans for the village.

118

Fig. 10.3 *Le Magasin à Maurice and The Maurice Historical Preservation Society Preservation of history has long been a concern to many people in the area. "Someone ought to save the old buildings," was commonly repeated. Only recently has there been a community effort in Maurice to establish a permanent non-profit society to accomplish their goal of capturing relics of their past.*

Members of the MHPS are pictured above (L-R): Richard Landry, Gerry LeBlanc, Janice Gary, Cheryl Broussard Perret, Douglas Villien, Debbie Broussard Choate, Gabby Broussard, Dr. Marc Villien, Dr. Richard Villien, Daniel Duhon and Francine Mathiew.

A plan to guide development was long overdue in Maurice when Mayor Ferguson coordinated assistance from Community Design Workshop of the University of Louisiana at Lafayette, School of Architecture and Design, to develop a comprehensive plan for the town.

Fig. 10.4
Existing Land Use Map of Maurice, 2009.

119

In 2009 the university initiated a land use study for the Village of Maurice including a series of community charettes. The workshop meetings identified present concerns and land use issues throughout the town. Consideration of implementing overlay districts was given specific attention to areas of town that clearly exhibit historical, cultural or economic value. The planning team recommended adopting an Overlay District Map as a guide to maintain essential characteristics of each district.

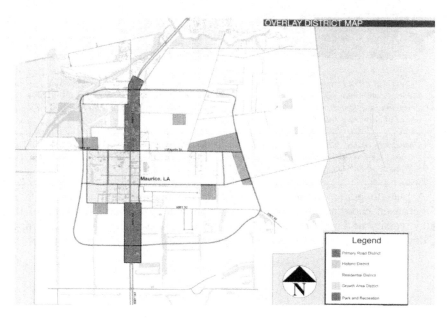

Fig. 10.5 Overlay District Map

The Community Design Workshop then published a comprehensive plan that included an overall vision for future land use. The report included transportation and Smart Growth Principles which are techniques and planning tools for implementation of the Master Plan. The plan made recommendations relating to land use, zoning, signage, creation of a Tax Increment Finance District and aesthetic improvements throughout the community. The Master Plan proposed by the Community Design Workshop anticipated accommodating a future population of 3000 people in Maurice.

Overall Vision

Being a small, rural community that wishes to preserve its character, increase quality of life for residents, and experience healthy growth, the masterplan maintains a compact, commercial town center with residential development radiating around it.

POPULATION: 3000

LEGEND
- Existing Structures
- Residential
- Commercial Office
- Commercial Retail
- Institutional

Fig. 10.6 *Future Land Use Plan of Maurice*

In April 2010 the U.S. Bureau of Census conducted the decennial census of population as mandated by the United States Constitution. Mayor Ferguson had hoped the population of Maurice increased to more than one thousand persons in the 2010 count. This would have elevated the status of Maurice from "Village" to "Town." The final result was released by the Census Bureau in April 2011. The long anticipated goal to attain one thousand persons had fallen short by thirty-six. Maurice will keep the designation of "Village" until the year 2020.

Maurice is comprised of a unique combination of history, tradition, cuisine and folklore embraced by a host of proud Cajuns. Villagers here anticipate future growth will go beyond existing boundaries but if not, many will be content to have Maurice remain *between the crossroads.*

Fig. B.1 *Mont Blanc from the Leon Villien alpage on the French-Italian border—
Vallon de Glaciers, Col de la Seigne and Mont Blanc.*

Biographical

Noted Persons. *Biographical information included here, relates to those who have left an impression either by their position in society or by their enduring contribution to history of the Village of Maurice. The following information has been secured either by most reliable sources available including the individual or persons who represent the subject. It is unfortunate that some persons were omitted due to lack of available information at the time of this writing. It is hoped that this work serves as a beginning and lasting testament to those who are represented. In the matter of those who were omitted, every effort will be made to acquire information about individuals for future publications. The publisher and author disclaim any responsibility as to the materials contained herein.*

Merchant, Planter and Founder

Jean-Maurice Villien was born January 17, 1831 in the commune of Bourg St-Maurice, in the hamlet of Vulmix, in the French-speaking area of the Savoie region of the Alps in the Kingdom of Sardinia (now part of France). He was Sardinian (Sard in French). Maurice (Jean-Maurice) was the son of Joseph Antoine Villien and Marie Angelique Miedan-Gros. Maurice had one sister and three brothers; Marie Adelaide, Joseph Etienne, Gaspard and Jacques-Marie.

Fig. B.2
Jean-Maurice Villien,
1831 – 1902

Jean-Maurice and Joseph-Etienne among other hyphenated surnames recurred in the Villien family through many decades. Sentiment of their homeland was brought to America: "Nous les Savoyarde sommes sensible a tout ce qui rappelle notre pays l'origine" (we, the Savoyards seem sensitive to any and everything which reminds us of our country of origin). The brothers hoped to seek out new opportunities in America and settle in an area that reminded them of their homeland. The city of New Orleans and Louisiana consisted of a large French-speaking population that was measurable enough to fill their ambition.

Maurice and Étienne were descendants of dairy farmers who were known for a variety of cheeses. Bourg St-Maurice was the largest town in the Tarentaise Valley within the heart of what is now the French Alps. Bourg St-Maurice was described as a peaceful little market town located in a large basin at a confluence of several valleys about 20 miles from the foot of Mt. Blanc. Cattle farming and cheese making was a major business activity in Bourg St. Maurice.

Maurice (age 24) and Étienne (age 27) left Bourg St-Maurice Maurice in 1855. When they departed their homeland, they were subjects of Charles Albert, King of Sardinia. The status of their citizenship changed while in the United States. They became naturalized French subjects of Napoléon III by French referendum annexing La Savoie to France in 1860. For Maurice, the status of being a naturalized citizen of France would become an important legal issue later in his life.

The brothers arrived by steamship in New Orleans in 1855. Maurice worked as a cobbler "cordonnier" during his time in New Orleans. While in New Orleans, Étienne died by accidental drowning in the Mississippi River. Maurice moved away from the busy

Fig. B.3
Joseph-Etienne and Jean-Maurice, ca. 1855

port city of New Orleans to the flat coastal bayou land of south Louisiana. A region that was vastly different from his home-life in the highest mountains of Europe. His quiet demeanor and loss of his only relative in America may have been overwhelming and compelling causes for moving to a tranquil rural environment similar to his home-life in Savoie. He was described by his son, Dr. J.A. Villien as mild mannered gentile, quiet and soft spoken. He was a small bearded man and never very talkative. He enjoyed a half strength glass of wine with his meals.

French-speaking people of Acadian and French descent were an established majority in south Louisiana. A district known as Attakapas included St. Martin, St. Mary, Lafayette, Vermilion and Iberia parishes. The Teche valley, a busy commercial corridor, provided comfort and opportunity for foreign French and other French-speaking immigrants. It was here in the Teche valley in ca. 1858, an area along the *Grand Marais* between Jeanerette and New Iberia where he began a new occupation as a traveling salesman, *colporteur*. For the time being, his occupation was relegated to selling wares from a wagon or hack and operating a small store he called *le petite magasin*.

By April, 1861, Maurice established residence not far from Bayou Teche, near a sugar plantation owned by the Patout family which later became known as Enterprise Plantation. The place name was *l'Île Piquante* [sic]. Later, the settlement of *Île Piquant* changed to Patoutville taking the name from the Patout family. The Enterprise Plantation was about four miles west of Jeanerette.

Like other foreign-French, Maurice was politically inactive and indifferent to the North and South discord. He had no interest in becoming involved with Southern rights or slaves. He was an energetic young man who engaged in marketing wares throughout the Teche and Vermilion area. He thought he was protected as a citizen of France and immune to engagement with union or confederate troops. He disagreed with the encroachment of the Civil War into his daily life. Unlike many who feared for their lives, he did not conscribe to either army.

In the autumn of 1863 "Les troupes fédérales" (federal troops), under direction of General Nathaniel P. Banks Union Army of the Gulf, canvassed the entire Teche-Vermilion region. His army flagrantly taking what they needed from homes and farms for their war effort. Concurrently destroying, burning, slaughtering livestock and leaving to waste what they could not take with them. Maurice soon found himself as victim of the army's wanton and greed. The XIII Army Corps, led by Maj. Gen. C.C. Washburn, and 1st Division. Brig. Gen. Michael K. Lawler with four infantry and one artillery group sent daily patrols from their encampment near Carlin plantation. On October 15 and 16, 1863 Maurice's Store and farm was pilfered of his possessions. The neighboring Patout family home and sugar plantation, managed by Mme. Appoline Fournier Patout and widow of Pierre Simeon Patout, was also looted and occupied by Union troops.

A patrol of ten soldiers entered his property and took items as small as sewing needles and cloth. Pigs (some of which were slaughtered on the spot in front of witnesses), many chickens, geese and ducks. An exhaustive list of items were taken from his store and living quarters (including employees' personal possessions) but of his most valuable of possessions were his horses displaying brands of legal identification.

Maurice filed claim in New Orleans on July 12, 1865 and presented a materials list of items taken by the union troops in October 1863. The claim was presented to the French-American Claims Commission.

> *"Que dans le mois d'octobre 1863, le comparant a vu les troupes fédérales alors de passage à "l'Île Piquante" (sur le Bayou Têche) prendre un cheval créole, bai âgé de 7 ans present ZT, la propriété du dit Jean Maurice Villien."*

> ("That in the month of October 1863, the witness saw the Federal troops while passing by "l'Île Piquante" (on Bayou Têche) take a créole, bay horse 7 years old, marked (branded) "ZT", the property of the said Jean-Maurice Villien.").

"Qu'ils connaissaient tous deux la jument de couleur jaunâtre present HS et propriété de Jean Maurice Villien que Mousieur Durocher l'a vu dans le camp des États-Unis et que Monsieur Simon Céler était present au moment ou elle a été requise par les forces des États-Unis".

"That both (witnesses) knew the yellowish mare marked (branded) "HS" and the property of Jean Maurice Villien and Mr. Durocher saw it in the U.S. Camp and Mr. Simon Céler was present at the time she was commandeered by the U.S. forces."

He subsequently was awarded compensation for damages and losses.

In August, 1866, he left l'Île Piquante and in ca. 1867, Maurice met Marie Chaty, daughter of Etienne Chaty and Christine Pelletier, in the course of his travels through Lafayette, Iberia and Vermilion parishes. Maurice and Marie were married in 1868. The Chaty family was native to Falquemont, France and lived in the Youngsville-Milton area.

Milton history denotes that in 1868 Maurice owned a trading post on the west side of Bayou Vermilion at Milton. It was the only store on the west side of the bayou. From there, Maurice continued to sell his wares by horse drawn hack. Not very long after establishing a depot at Milton, Maurice and Marie re-established a home and store in an area three miles west of Milton on the high prairie, *Prairie Vermilion*. They became pioneers of commerce situated along a meandering wagon road that traversed across the prairie. The land was owned by the government and yet unclaimed. The home site was in a small island of trees, a grove, on a sea of grassland in Section 11 (T11S, R3E).

First records of Maurice and Marie Chaty Villien's home and mercantile in Vermilion Parish was that of the 1870 U.S. Census, church records of St. Mary Magdalen and then an application for a land grant in 1873. Family history recalls the name of their store on the prairie as "le Magasin à Maurice."

Fig. B.4 *Prairie Vermilion*
Today some areas of the prairie around Maurice have similar appearance to the era when it was first visited by Jean-Maurice Villien.

While living at the grove, Maurice and Marie had five children, Joseph Angelle (July 20, 1870) and Jean Maurice, Jr. (February 24, 1875) lived to adulthood. Both sons were educated at St. Charles College in Grand Coteau and became prominent figures in the future of Maurice. In 1875 Maurice was granted citizenship of the United States of America.

By the 1880's he was a successful merchant and planter. His farming business had become sizeable and he primarily traded in cattle, cotton and rice.

Maurice and Marie, being devout Catholics, built a church in 1886 on a ten acre tract carved from their quarter section of land. In 1889 the name of the first church was accepted as "Église de St. Alphonse à Mauriceville." St. Alphonse Catholic Church is the second oldest Catholic Church in Vermilion Parish.

In 1893 he unveiled plans and advertised for the sale of lots. He partnered with businesswoman, Corine Broussard to form fourteen blocks for a town layout. In circa 1894 Maurice moved the mercantile business and his home from the grove to the more accessible site located on Maurice Avenue, a street named for him.

The United States Postal Service established a Post Office within his mercantile on September 19, 1895. The community was called Mauriceville by area residents and consisted of approximately 50 people. Maurice simplified the post mark and designated the post office with his name "Maurice."

About the same period, Maurice also invested in land about ten miles west of Maurice (three miles north of Kaplan). A new community called Cossinade was growing. He hoped to capitalize by establishing another retail business there. His ambition to build another mercantile in the promising community fell short of implementation when Cossinade failed to grow as a community.

Maurice died on May 7, 1902 and in St. Alphonsus Church correspondence from Father Rochard to the diocesan officials, noted a name change in 1902 from Mauriceville to Maurice. Maurice's widow, Marie Chaty Villien, continued the family dairy and mercantile business with her sons Jean and Joseph.

Fig. B.5
Jean-Maurice Villien
memorial cards
Born January 17, 1831,
Died May 7, 1902
71 Years 3 Months   20 Days

127

A larger mercantile building was constructed by Marie Chaty Villien and their sons, Jean and Joseph, in ca. 1916 at the corner of Maurice Avenue and Church Street. The new store was named Villien Brothers and Company.

Marie Villien continued to reside in the home on Maurice Avenue, adjacent to the bank, until her death in 1932.

Fig. B.6 Home of Dr. Joseph A. Villien, Sr.

Mayor, Physician, Businessman, Banker and Farmer

Dr. Joseph A. Villien, Sr. was born July 20, 1870 and was the eldest of two sons of Jean-Maurice and Marie Chaty Villien. His brother, Jean (John) Maurice Villien, Jr. was born in 1875. They were born at "The Grove" on their father's homestead. Joseph was educated at St. Charles College in Grand Coteau and graduated with a Bachelor of Arts degree in 1887. He continued on to medical college at Tulane University in New Orleans where he graduated in 1890. Upon completion of medical college, Dr. Villien began practicing medicine in the community of Milton as an associate of Dr. Milton R. Cushman. They were the only two doctors in Milton.

Fig. B.7
Dr. J.A. Villien, Sr.,
1870 – 1958

He was a member of the Attakapas Medical Association and was financial secretary of that organization in 1891. His brother John also attended school at St. Charles College in 1892.

Dr. Villien married Octavie Broussard on April 24, 1895. Dr. Villien moved his practice to Maurice and built a home on a ten site carved from his father's homestead. The home site was at the west end of Joseph Street. The Victorian styled house was a focal point of the Villien farm and one of the largest homes in the area. His marriage to Octavie Broussard gave birth to eight children; Andre L., Brice, Jacques Cyr, Albert Armel, Lastie Maurice, Rita Marie, Ferdinand Opta, and Angelle Perpetue. Octavie (b. January 6, 1874) died August 12, 1907. She was the daughter of Lastie Broussard and Perpetue Mayard of Abbeville.

Joseph and Octavie Villien were active parishioners at St. Alphonsus Catholic Church and in 1904 helped construct a new church building which replaced the one built by his father, Maurice Villien.

As planter and businessman of Vermilion Parish his notoriety was known throughout southwest Louisiana. His large farm consisted of several hundred acres. The farm once grazed several hundred cattle, harvested rice, corn, sweet potatoes, cotton, and other crops.

Dr. Villien married Annette Maude Gaidry, his second wife, on March 19, 1915. She was the daughter of John Dreux and Philomene Rouen Gaidry, natives of Montegut in Terrebonne Parish. Maude was a teacher at Maurice School from 1913 to 1914. Dr. Villien and Maude gave birth to seven children; Joseph Angelle, Jr., John Drew, Paul Ovide, George Carrol, Louise Anne and Alfred Carl.

Dr. Villien was a physician, merchant, mayor, planter, post master, banker and philanthropist. He was active in Knights of Columbus and served on the financial committee of the Abbeville Chamber of Commerce.

He practiced medicine in Maurice until he retired in 1920. He continued to serve as postmaster from 1902 to 1912. The post office was first in "le Magasin à Maurice" and the Villien Brothers and Company mercantile buildings owned by the Villien family.

The Franklin and Abbeville Railroad was constructed from New Iberia to Milton in 1910. Construction of the railroad was successful through the efforts of Dr. J.A. Villien, A.B. Daniels, Exalt Prejean, Lovelace Boudreaux, and Dr. A.J. Burkett. The rail line operated until 1930 when the state began to pave many of the state and parish roads.

The town of Maurice was incorporated on December 27, 1911 and was officially named the Village of Maurice. Dr. Villien served as the first mayor of Maurice from January 1912 to December 1920 and a member of the Vermilion Parish School Board from 1906 to 1914. His interests in expanding the Villien Brothers further broadened into partnership with the Maurice Cotton Gin, Co. where he served as secretary and treasurer until 1951.

In 1918 the capacity of St. Alphonsus Church had become inadequate. Again, Dr. and Mrs. Villien contributed to the construction of the third church which was built in 1918. This building continued in use until 1969 when the fourth church building was constructed. The fourth church building is in use today on the original site donated by his father.

Dr. Villien founded the independent Bank of Maurice in 1920 and on February 17, 1954 in one of the most talked about regional bank heists of the century, a lone bank robber entered the bank killing the teller and seriously wounding Dr. Villien. He continued to work at the Maurice bank after the robbery until his death in 1958. His wife, Maude G. Villien died May 11, 1992.

Businesswoman

Corine Marie Broussard was seventh generation Acadian descent from Jean Francois Broussard. She was the daughter of Camille Jean Francois Broussard (descendant of Jean Francois Baptiste Broussard and Hortense Broussard of St. Martinville) and Aurelia Emelia Broussard (daughter of Edouard Broussard and Euphemie Sylvanie Broussard). Four siblings, Corine M., Maria, Jean Treville and Albert inherited significant acreage located in section twelve (the southeast quadrant of Maurice) from their parents, Camille J.F. and Aurelia E. Broussard. Camille Jean Francois Broussard homesteaded the southwest quarter of section twelve (one hundred sixty-one acres).

Fig. B.8
Corine Marie Broussard,
1867 – 1945

Prior to her marriage to Hilaire Broussard in 1895, Corine partnered with Jean Maurice Villien and followed a subdivision plan to sell lots for commercial and residential use. Advertisement for lots appeared in early 1885. The two proprietors began to implement the plan envisioned by Maurice Villien. Land records indicate that Corine and Maurice exchanged properties at some point during the partnership because each of them had title to land in the other's original section.

130

Corine married Hilaire [sic] Broussard and constructed a prominent home and store on the northeast corner of Maurice Avenue and Church Street. Corine was known for contributions to the Church, school and community. Corine and Hilaire had six children but often took in orphans and boarders. Maude Gaidry, one of the first teachers at Maurice, boarded there in 1914. The parlor in the Broussard house was also used for funeral wakes.

After their store went out of business, it was converted into a moving picture theater before it was dismantled. Corine died December 23, 1945.

Merchant
Hilaire Darmas Broussard was born July 13, 1872 in Lafayette Parish. He was one of six children of Darmas Broussard and Sarah Jane Lyons. His siblings were Anastasie, Eloi, Joseph, Marie Melanie and Benjamin. The Broussard family was one of the largest land owners in the Lafayette, Youngsville and Milton area. Hilaire received an education in Bay St. Louis before returning to the area. In 1895 he married Corine M. Broussard of Maurice and established a mercantile on the site of their home at the corner of Maurice Avenue and Church Street. He served as Alderman of Maurice from 1912 to 1914. He died October 12, 1964.

Fig. B.9
Hilaire D. Broussard,
1872 – 1964

Merchant, Businessman
Jean Camille Broussard was eighth generation Cajun and descendant of Jean Francois Broussard. He was one of eight children of Albert Broussard and Marie Leocadie Nunez. Jean Camille was known as "Camille or Tee Camille". He was born May 2, 1890 on the family dairy farm near Maurice and attended Maurice Elementary. When he was ten years old he moved in with his aunt and uncle Corine and Hilaire Broussard of Maurice. He later lived with his great aunt Clophe Broussard in Lafayette where he attended school. He moved back to Maurice and became employed at Villien Brothers Store where he learned the skills of mercantile. He had a passion to become a merchant and avoided encouragement of working in the family's successful farming and cattle business.

Fig. B.10
Jean Camille Broussard,
1890 – 1938

He acquired possession of Broussard's Store established by his father Albert and within a short period of time entered into business partnership with his brother-in-law, Adonis Picard. By their partnership the name of the store was changed to Broussard-Picard Store. It was located on Maurice Avenue between Broussard and Joseph Street.

Camille married Ada Hebert in 1916. Ada was the daughter of Lastie Hebert and Marie Fabre. Camille and Ada had eleven children: Edward and Doris, Lastie, Claude, Wallace, Gladys, John, Alice, Willie, Walter and Faye Marie. Business partner, Adonis Picard, was the son of Aristide Picard and Azema Broussard. Aristide and Azema had twelve children. He was a saloon owner on Maurice Avenue.

Camille was a devout Catholic and active parishioner at St. Alphonsus Catholic Church. He was also active in civic affairs and served as alderman for Maurice from 1916 to 1919. He died on February 3, 1938. Ada and their oldest son, J. Edward, continued the partnership with Adonis Picard until the business closed.

Businessman
Ernest G. Trahan was a native of Judice. Ernest was the son of Gustave and Azemie Simon Trahan of Lafayette. Ernest married Laura Trahan of Maurice. Laura was the daughter of Cyprien D. and Felicia Cormier Trahan who were natives of Lafayette and moved to Maurice in 1898.

Ernest and his father, Cyprien, purchased the City Bar from Felix Nugent in ca. 1927. The father and son team managed the business icon until their deaths in November 1950.

Fig. B.11
Ernest G. Trahan
1898 - 1950

Mayor and Physician

Dr. Carroll J. Mouton was born June 6, 1899 and was a native of Lafayette. He was the son of David Mouton and Ida Campbell. Dr. Mouton was a graduate of St. Charles College in Grand Coteau and Tulane University School of Medicine in New Orleans. He married Anna Nugent and they resided in Maurice from 1921 to 1949. He established an office and practiced medicine in Maurice during the same period until his retirement in June 1949. He was active as a third degree Knights of Columbus (#1286/Laf.) and served as mayor of Maurice from 1928 to 1949. He then moved to Judice with his wife Anna Nugent Mouton and one daughter, Anna Grace "Putsie" Mouton. "Putsie" married George C. Villien, Sr., son of Dr. J.A.

Fig. B.12
Dr. Carroll J. Mouton
1899 – 1980

Villien of Maurice. George and Putsie Villien had four children: Martha V. Bunnell, George C. "Buzzy" Villien, Jr., Carroll J. Villien and David Villien.

Principal and Educator

Romain Picard was a native of Vermilion Parish. He was the son of Augustin Picard and Eliza Denais, and grandson of Aristide and Azema Broussard who owned a business in Maurice. Adonis, a brother of Augustin, opened a prominent business in Maurice, Broussard-Picard General Merchandise. Romain had five siblings, Jill, Esson, Avenal, Oza and Jeanne. He grew up on a farm south of Maurice. Romain attended Milton School and then Southwestern Louisiana Institute where he played football (six-man), ran track and graduated with a degree in education.

Fig. B.13
Romain Picard
1909 – 1966

Romain married Evangeline Martin of Lafayette Parish had two children, Cecil and Geraldine.

He was principal, teacher and coach at LeLeux Elementary School near Kaplan for eleven years prior to becoming principal at Maurice High School. He served as principal at Maurice High School from 1942 to 1966. His son, Cecil, succeeded him as principal in 1967.

133

Government Leader, Principal and Educator

Cecil Picard was the great-grandson of Aristide (from France) and Azema Broussard Picard of the Maurice-Milton community (Ward Four). Aristide owned a general store at Maurice. Aristide and Azema had twelve children. Augustin, the oldest child married Eliza Denais and lived in Maurice. Augustin and Eliza had six children, the oldest was Romain Picard principal of Maurice Elementary and father of Cecil Picard.

Fig. B.14
Cecil J. Picard
1938 -2007

Cecil Picard was born January 1, 1938 to the late Romain and Evangeline Martin Picard. He grew up in Maurice, attended Maurice Elementary while his father was principal there. Cecil graduated from Maurice High School and received a degree in Upper Elementary Education from Southwestern Louisiana Institute, which later became the University of Southwestern Louisiana and then the University of Louisiana at Lafayette. He earned a Master of Arts degree in Administration and Supervision from Sam Houston State Teachers College in Huntsville, Texas. Cecil Picard married Gaylen David of Abbeville and had two sons, Layne and Tyron.

After college, Cecil immediately began teaching at LeBlanc Elementary School in Erath and in 1962 he became a teacher and coach at Maurice High School. After his father's death in 1969 he filled his father's position as principal. He served as principal of Maurice High School for 11 years. He retired as principal and he was elected to the Louisiana House of Representatives in 1976. His first full term in the Senate was in 1979. He served in the House from 1975 – 1979. He served in the Senate from 1979 - 1992 and from 1992 – 1996.

As a member of the Senate, Picard was lead author of more than 50 pieces of legislation and championed numerous education reform initiatives aimed at improving education in Louisiana, including the Educational Employees Professional Improvement Program (1980), the law requiring mandatory kindergarten (1984), the Children First Act (1988) and the law creating Louisiana's first Early Childhood Opportunity Program (1992).

In 1996 he was named Superintendent of Education for the state of Louisiana. In 2005 Cecil was credited for his enormous contributions and involvement in establishing the Child Development Center, now the "Cecil J. Picard Center for Child Development." The name of Maurice Elementary was changed to Cecil J. Picard Elementary School at Maurice following his death in 2007.

Cecil is credited for developing Louisiana's Accountability Program which ranked number one in the nation by *Education Week* magazine, and for creating Louisiana's pre-K program for at-risk students, LA 4, now a model for the nation in early childhood education. His contributions have been a positive influence in education in Louisiana. He was a native of Maurice who served as a teacher, coach, principal, State Representative, State Senator, and one of the state's top educational leaders.

Mayor and Businessman

Corbette A. LeBlanc, Sr., son of Martin and Louise Arnaune LeBlanc was born on January 25, 1899 at their home near Coulee Kinney in north Vermilion Parish. Corbette attended school in Abbeville and as a young man worked at his family owned dairy located south of Maurice. He married Cecile Essie Broussard of Maurice in 1920 and lived in an apartment above the Broussard-Picard General Store. Corbette and Cecile later moved in with his mother-in-law, Aminthe, her home was on the corner of Maurice Avenue and W. Joseph Street. The house was the former home of Jean (John) and Aminthe Villien and still stands on that corner as a prominent historic structure of Maurice.

Fig. B.15
Corbette A. LeBlanc, Sr.
1899 – 1991

Corbette was proud to be a citizen of Maurice and proud of his French heritage. Both of his parents were from France where he had the opportunity to visit their home towns during the summer of 1981.

He was employed many years at Villien Brother's store in Maurice, later he established his own store, C. A. LeBlanc General Merchandise, located at the corner of Maurice Avenue and Corine Street. His business was in operation for thirty-three years until it closed in the mid-1960's. The building stands today and is owned by his granddaughter, Jacqueline L. Truitt.

Corbette was always active and had a sincere interest in civic affairs and local politics. He served as a councilman of Maurice from 1958 to 1962.

He was elected mayor in 1962 and served the residents of Maurice for five consecutive terms. He was very well respected in Maurice because of his ability to serve the needs of the community and to work with the councils. Corbette was credited for construction of the first City Hall, a fire house, and establishment of city water and sewage.

One of his greatest achievements during his term of office was working with Governor Edwin Edwards on bringing the four-lane highway through Maurice. Louisiana state officials proposed a by-pass away from the center of town.

Mayor LeBlanc was awarded honorary status by the Louisiana State Legislature as State Representative in 1977 and State Senator in 1978.

Corbette and Cecile had one son, Corbett A. LeBlanc, Jr. and two grand-daughters, Jacqueline L. Truitt of Lafayette and Sonia L. Comboy of Maurice. Corbette LeBlanc retired in 1982 and died January 1, 1991.

Dentist, Preservationist, Philanthropist and Historian
Dr. Paul O. Villien, Sr. was the son of Dr. Joseph A. Villien, Sr. and Annette Maude Gaidry Villien of Maurice. Dr. Villien, a native of Maurice, was born February 10, 1922 and was known as "Polo" by family, friends and teachers. He attended Maurice Elementary School from first grade through seventh grade. He attended Cathedral High School in Lafayette from eighth grade through tenth grade. From 1937 to 1938 he attended and graduated Jefferson Military College at Washington, Mississippi. Then attended Spring Hill College, Pre-Dental School, Mobile, Alabama from 1938 to 1941. While at Mobile, he received his private pilot license and training at Bates Air Field. From 1941 to 1944 he attended Loyola Dental

Fig. B.16
Dr. Paul O. Villien, Sr.
1922 – 2006

School in New Orleans where he graduated with honors in Dentistry. In June 1944 he married Lucille "Tookoo" Lewis, daughter of John W. Lewis, Jr. and Ruth Carrol West of Lafayette. Mrs. Villien is descendant of Judge Seth Lewis and Richard West settlers and statesmen of St. Landry and Calcasieu parishes.

In 1944 Dr. Villien was commissioned as a Lieutenant in the U.S. Naval Reserve and served at Parris Island, South Carolina at the Marine Barrack Dental Dispensary. He also served at Vanderbilt University Naval ROTC in the V-12 Unit in Nashville, Tennessee, Chapel Hill University Medical Hospital, Chapel Hill, South Carolina, and Duke University, Durham, North Carolina. He had a private dental practice in Abbeville from 1947 to 1992. He was a charter member of the Dental Society, Third District of Louisiana, a member of the American Dental Society, Acadiana Dental Society, Junior Chamber of Commerce and the Abbeville Kiwanis Club.

Dr. Villien's interest in genealogy and preservation of family history was significant in unraveling decades of archival data and memorabilia. His unyielding research and collection of information was relevant to the founder, Jean-Maurice Villien and to the history of the Village of Maurice. Detailed descriptions of his contributions were provided in recent publications by Dr. Paul O. Villien, Jr., *Villien-Chaty family...et nos aieux, Volumes I and II.*

Through his diligence family bonds were established with French cousins and renewed with local families at a large gathering in Maurice in 2009. A fete of such confluence rarely occurs in researching family history.

Dr. and Mrs. Paul Villien had seven children: Suzanne V. Cassedy, Augusta, Georgia, Dr. Paul O. Villien, Jr., New Orleans, Louisiana, Douglas L. Villien, Sr., Baton Rouge, Louisiana, Dr. Richard P. Villien, Lafayette, Louisiana, Thomas J. Villien, Charlottesville, Virginia, Dr. Marc J. Villien, Maurice, Louisiana, and Yvette V. Bethea, Baton Rouge, Louisiana. Dr. Villien died November 27, 2006.

Educator, Raconteur and Church Volunteer

Rose Rachel Martin Villien, was a native of Carencro and born in 1897. Her parents were Joseph Claude and Alida Martin of Carencro. She was the oldest of four children. The Martin family was a descendant of Andre Martin and Jean Mouton, early settlers of Lafayette Parish. Her grandfather, Edgar Martin, was the first Superintendent of Schools in Lafayette Parish, so it was no wonder that Rachel pursued a degree in teaching. Mrs. Villien was married 42 years to the late Jacques "Jack" Cyr Villien of Maurice (d. 1962). Jack was the son of Dr. J.A. Villien, Sr. Jeanne Arlene was the only child of Jack and Rachel's marriage. Arlene was a teacher in Donaldsonville and Napoleonville before she married Dr. Thomas A. Wynne of Sierra Madre, California. Her grandchildren are: Catherine Wynne, Thomas Wynne, Margaret Wynne and James Wynne.

Fig. B.17
Rachel Martin Villien
1897 – 2005

She graduated from Southwestern Louisiana Institute in 1918. Mrs. Villien taught school at Maurice Elementary for 39 years before retiring in 1961. She had taught first grade to almost every adult in Maurice over the age of 40 in 1997. She was a natural story teller and loved talking to anyone who would listen to her. Her contributions in Maurice will live on for generations through the grade school students she taught.

Mrs. Villien was a member of the Ladies Altar Society at St. Alphonsus Catholic Church.

In a grand ceremony provided by residents of Maurice celebrating her 100 years of age, August 30, 1997 was proclaimed Rachel Villien Day in Maurice. Nason Trahan, Alderman, presented the award telling that she had taught him first grade. She was also presented an award by Cecil Picard, former Louisiana State Superintendent of Schools, who had been her first grade pupil, and an award from the State Legislature. An article in the Lafayette Advertiser on August 30, 2002 summarized Rachel as a "105-year-old walking, talking history book."

Former principal, Patricia "Pat" Webb memorializes Rachel's humor each time that she recounts a favorite moment at Maurice Elementary. "Ms. Rachel was brought to school to visit when she was 100 plus years. I was told she was hard of hearing, and to talk loud to her. It was lunch time, so we put her sitting in the cafeteria so she could see the students. She watched each class enter with a smile on her face, but, when our special needs class entered, she watched with even more interest. I know when she was a teacher, special needs students were not on campus. As she watched the wheelchairs enter, I bent down and said, in a loud voice, "these are our special needs students that I love very much" ....she looked up at me with a twisted look on her face and said to me" I'm old, NOT DEAF" Two teachers sitting at her table had to get up and leave they were laughing so much and as they walked away, one said to me, "I've never heard anybody tell you off that way".................it was wonderful meeting her that day."

Mrs. Villien died in 2005 and at the time of her death was the oldest living alumna from Southwestern Louisiana Institute (USL/ULL).

Postmaster, Businessman
Cyprien D. Trahan, a native of Lafayette was born on September 10, 1879 and the youngest of nine children of Onesime D. Trahan and Marie Genevieve Leger. He married Felicia Cormier in 1898 in Maurice. Felicia was the daughter of Simeon Cormier and Octavia Guillot of Lafayette. Cyprien and Felicia had one child, Laura, who was born in Maurice in 1899. Laura Street in Maurice was named after her. Laura married Ernest G. Trahan of Judice. They resided in Maurice and had four children, Warren Cyprien, Charles Ernest, Robert Lee and Harold G.

Fig.B.18
Cyprien D. Trahan
1879 – 1950

In January 1905 Cyprien became a Notary Public in Maurice and in 1913 became postmaster. He served as postmaster until 1946. On December 27, 1913, he was dually appointed the first Secretary Pro Tem for the Village of Maurice. He served as Secretary or Clerk until 1920. Around 1916 he became employed at Villien Brothers General Merchandise and by 1917 entered into partnership at Villien Brothers with Dr. J.A. Villien and Jean "John" Villien.

138

Cyprien was very active with St. Alphonsus Catholic Church and served on committees as well as a member of the board. In 1920 he was named by Father Louis Laroche, "godfather of the bell" at St. Alphonsus. In 1925 he served as President and founding member of the board of the Maurice Cotton Gin Company. Around 1928 he purchased Maurice City Bar from Felix Nugent and he was a founding proprietor in the Trahan Rice Mill and Seed Company. Cyprien died on November 6, 1950, while living in Maurice.

Businessman, Farmer

James "Jack" Cyr Villien was born July 10, 1898 and was a second generation Villien in America. He was the third of eight children of Dr. Joseph A. Villien and Octavie Broussard. Only five of the children lived to adulthood. Following his education at St. Charles College at Grand Coteau, he married Rose Rachel Martin of Carencro and returned to Maurice to manage his father's complex farming operation. He was a charter member in Vermilion Parish and the Louisiana Farm Bureau Federation. He served as president of Vermilion Parish Farm Bureau and Vice President of the Louisiana State Farm Bureau. Jack Villien died January 14, 1962.

Fig. B.19
James Cyr Villien
1898 – 1962

Jack and Rachel had one child, Jeanne Arline Villien Wynne. Arline married Dr. Thomas A. Wynne of Sierra Madre, California. Arline and Thomas had four children: James M., Margaret J., Thomas A. and Catherine.

Educator, Librarian, Civic and Church Volunteer

Alberta "Berta" Villien Winch, a native of Maurice, was born December 21, 1928. She was the daughter of Albert Armel Villien and Pearl Margaret Steen. Albert and Pearl had three children, Phro Margaret, Alberta Octavia and Yvonne Rita. She graduated valedictorian from Maurice High School in 1946. She attended University of Louisiana at Lafayette (then Southwestern Louisiana Institute) in 1950. She majored in education and received degrees English, Social Studies and Library Science. She served as Librarian and taught English at Maurice High School from 1950 to 1951.

Fig. B.20
Alberta Octavia Villien Winch
1928 -

Berta married Luther Lewis Winch, Jr. in 1950. Luther was a native of Pecan Island. Berta attended Louisiana State University and received her master's degree in Library Science in 1958.

She returned to Maurice to teach and serve as librarian from 1958 to 1988. In 1966 the Maurice School yearbook, *Bow Wow,* was dedicated in her honor. In 1974 she served on St. Alphonsus Parish Church Council and was a member of Catholic Daughters and Ladies Altar Society. She also served as Formation Director in 1994 and Prioress of Abbeville Lay Carmelites from 1965 to 1966. Berta and Luther had one daughter, Barbara Anne House of Baton Rouge.

Berta is a member of the Louisiana Library Association, Vermilion Parish Library Association, Louisiana Retired Teachers Association, Vermilion Retired Teachers Association, "Delta Kappa Gamma," and "Beta Phi Mu."

She is recognized as a librarian, teacher, historian and friend. Her contributions centered on genealogy and preservation of Maurice history. Her knowledge of history can be traced to recent publications of the *History of St. Alphonsus Catholic Church*, *History of Vermilion Parish* publish by the *Vermilion Historical Society* and the *Attakapas Gazette* published by the *Attakapas Historical Association.*

Businessman, Fireman

Henri Fred Broussard, son of Ducré Broussard and Olive Trahan was born on January 2, 1930 and grew up in Maurice. Fred attended first through eleventh grade at Maurice High School and graduated in 1946. During his youth he worked at Villien Brothers. He first learned his electrical trade by working evening hours with Mr. Albert Villien and Mr. Whitney Vincent. After returning from serving his country, he worked with his father and brothers at Dixie Autolec. Fred married Elodie "Lou" Hebert of Kaplan, LA in 1951 and remained in Maurice for his entire life. Fred and Lou had four children, Marlene, Catherine, Margaret and Timothy. All four children still live in Maurice.

Fig. B.21
Chief H. Fred Broussard
1930 – 1999

In 1966, Fred and his brothers Will, Raymond and Roderick decided to remain in Maurice. Each established their own businesses in the community. The oldest brother, Will opened a grocery and hardware store, Raymond established an appliance service center and the youngest brother, Roderick, repaired television and radios. His sister Joyce B. Gauthier taught at Maurice High School until she retired.

Fred established an independent regional plumbing, electrical and air conditioning service located on James Street. He was proud of his occupation and his service in helping others but most of all "he lived for the fire department." He was one of the founding fathers of the Maurice Volunteer Fire Department and served many years as chief of the department.

Fred died suddenly while fighting an intense fire at a local service station south of Maurice. Chief Broussard was recognized and honored in 1999 by the National Volunteer Firefighters Council and the National Fallen Firefighters Foundation.

Businessman

Albert Armel Villien, a native of Maurice, was born April 12, 1900. He was the second son of Dr. Joseph A. Villien and Octavia Broussard. He married Pearl Margaret Steen (b. 1902), a native of Iota and resided most of his life in Maurice. Albert attended elementary and high school at St Charles Academy in Grand Coteau. He continued his education at Southwestern Louisiana Institute in Lafayette where he lettered in baseball. He later attended Tyler

Fig. B.22
Albert Armel Villien
1900 – 1983

Business College and moved to Iota where he clerked at a general store. There he met his bride, Pearl Steen. They moved to Maurice ca. 1922 and he clerked at his father's store, Villien Brothers. In 1923, he established Maurice Garage but continued to clerk at Villien Brothers. He was also a skilled electrician and wired many buildings throughout the community. He later went to work for Wood Motors and then Bay City Motors in Abbeville. Albert was dedicated to making Maurice a better place and served eight years as an Alderman from 1966 to 1974. Albert died on July 7, 1983. Albert and Pearl had three children: Phro Margaret, married to Roy M. Moss; Alberta Octavia, married to Luther Lewis Winch; and Yvonne Rita, married to Cecil L. Culver, Jr.

Mayor

Barbara Landry Picard was born September 20, 1930 in Delcambre. She is the daughter of Ollie and Bernadette Landry of Delcambre. She graduated from Delcambre High School in 1948 and attended Spencer Business College in Lafayette in 1950. Mrs. Picard married Paul J. Picard in 1950 then moved to Maurice. Mr. and Mrs. Picard had three children, Caroline, Douglas and Elizabeth. Mrs. Picard first worked as a clerk for Judge Richard Putnam of Abbeville, then became the first secretary at Maurice High School and North Vermilion High School. She served as alderman from 1975 to 1982 then as mayor until 2007.

Fig. B.23
Barbara L. Picard
1930 -

Mayor
Robert Harry "Bob" Ferguson was born November 10, 1946 in Maurice. He is the son of Edward and Jeanne Ferguson of Maurice. His mother, Jeanne, was the daughter of Robert and Amay Dartez. Robert Dartez was former Chief of Police for Maurice and night watchman of the Maurice Cotton Gin. Mr. Ferguson was raised in Maurice and moved back to Maurice after living in Beaumont, Texas. He attended Maurice Elementary and High School, the University of Southwestern Louisiana at Lafayette, and Delgado Community College in New Orleans. He received a degree in Business Management. He married the late Wanda Migues in 1966 and had three children, Michael, Dr. Amy Ferguson Lawrence, and Edward. He served in the U. S. Navy from 1964 to 1967. He was employed in the telecommunications industry for BellSouth, AT&T and Executone in New Iberia, Jeanerette, Abbeville, Lafayette, New Orleans, Atlanta and currently in Lafayette.

Fig. B.24
Robert H. Ferguson
1946 -

Mayor
Wayne Theriot was born July 3, 1950 in Abbeville and graduated from Vermilion Catholic High School in 1968. He graduated from the University of Southwestern Louisiana in 1972 receiving a Bachelor of Science in Business Administration. In May of 1973 he married Marlene Broussard and have four children and three grandchildren. Mr. and Mrs. Theriot moved to Maurice in 1979. Since that time he served sixteen years on the Board of Aldermen for the village as well as secretary for the Maurice Volunteer Fire Department, President of the Saint Alphonsus Church Council and Chairman of the Maurice Elementary Building Committee. He was also involved with community youth league recreation. He coached baseball and basketball. He retired in 2011 after serving as an administrator for 34 years at the University of Louisiana at Lafayette.

Fig. B.25
Wayne Theriot
1950 -

Businessman
Alexandre Bruce Mouton was born March 26, 1899. He was the fourth son of Fran G. Mouton and Leontine Doucet. He was a great-grandson of Governor Alexandre Mouton. He was a graduate of Simon College of Pharmacy at Tulane University. He moved to Maurice in 1927 and married Cleida Babin in 1928. Following her death in 1930, he married Lucille Wilkins, a teacher in Maurice, in 1932. He was a trustee at St. Alphonsus Church and a member of KC #1286. He was a member of the La. Pharmaceutical Assoc. and N.A.R.D., Vermilion Parish School Board, Vermilion Parish Draft Board and the Maurice Board of Aldermen. Bruce died June 16, 1987. He is survived by two daughters, Petesy Mouton Hernandez of Lafayette and Lynn Mouton Spence of Houston, Texas, and one son, A. Bruce Mouton, Jr. of Hot Springs, Arkansas.

Fig. B.26
A. Bruce Mouton
1899 -1987

142

Appendix

MAYORS

Dr. Joseph A. Villien, Sr.	1912
Dr. Carroll J. Mouton	1928
Dr. Harold G. Trahan	1949
Corbette A. LeBlanc, Sr.	1962
Barbara L. Picard	1982
Robert H. Ferguson	2007
Wayne Theriot	2011

RECREATIONAL DIRECTOR

Wallace P. Broussard	1967

SECRETARY – TREASURERS / ADMINISTRATOR

Cyprien D. Trahan	1912
Ernest G. Trahan	1920
Ernest Charles Trahan	1951
Homer Broussard, Sr.	1966
Willie A. Broussard	1969
Richard L. Hebert	1970
Willie A. Broussard	1970

BOOK KEEPER / CLERK

Gladu Montet	1951
G.B. LeBlanc	1966
Terry Broussard	1968
Richard L. Hebert	1969
Dudley Trahan	1974
Willie A. Broussard	1975
Mary Hebert	1995
Melanie Denais	2006
Joan D. Methvin	2011

LEGAL ADVISOR

George J. Bailey	1954
Nolan J. Sandoz	1962
Silas B. Cooper, Jr.	1966
	1974
Anthony Fontana	1974
Scott Dartez	2011
Calvin E. Woodruff, Jr.	1978
Scott Frazier	1992
Michael Landry	1998
Carl Robicheaux	1998
Calvin E. Woodruff	2003
Scott Dartez	2011

JUDGE OF THE MAGISTRATE

Calvin E. Woodruff, Jr.	1978
Ted Ayo	2011

PROSECUTOR

Bernard Duhon

VILLAGE ENGINEER

Gene Sellers	1974
Tim Mader	1974
Sellers & Associates	--

STREET COMMSSIONER

Elix Hebert	1954
Camille Hebert	1956
Eugene Broussard	1966
Claude Breaux	1970
David Villien	1999

TOWN MARSHALL / POLICE CHIEF

J. Hazard Broussard	1914 - 1918
J. Hazard Broussard	1926 - 1949
Henry A. Bacque	1918 - 1919
Edmund Richard	1920 – 1926
John Villien	1926 - 1928
Adler Vincent	1949 - 1950
Robert Dartez	1950 – 1962

Woodley Trahan	1962 - 1977
J.D. Spurgeon	1977 - 1979
Lenes "Steve" Schexnaider	1978 - 1981
Kenneth Beasley	1981 - 1981
Edwin Pratt	1981 - 1981
Dwain Rider	1981 - 1982
Warren Rost	1982 -

ALDERMEN OF MAURICE

Henry A. Bacque	1912 - 1926
Eraste Broussard	1912 - 1915
Hilaire D. Broussard	1912 - 1914
J. Avery Dartez	1914 - 1922
Felix Nugent	1915 - 1922
J. Camille Broussard	1916 - 1919
Hypolite Dronet	1916 - 1920
Eli(e) Vincent	1920 - 1924
Adonis Picard	1922 - 1942
Abraham Broussard	1924 - 1926
Edmond Richard	1926 - 1928
David Mouton	1926 - 1926
Jean (John) Villien	1928
Saul Broussard	1928 - 1946
Phillip E. Trahan	1928 - 1938
A. Bruce Mouton	1930 - 1946
Lannes Comeaux	1934 - 1942
Elix Hebert	1949 - 1958
Gabriel LeBlanc	1958 - 1962
Wilven Edward Hebert	1954 - 1974
Corbette A. LeBlanc	1954 - 1958
Camille Hebert	1958 - 1962
Phillip Montet	1962 - 1966
Lester Gauthier	1966 - 1974
Fidney Trahan	1966 - 1970
Albert A. Villien	1966 - 1974
Edward Hebert	1970 - 1974
Jean Dudley Trahan	1974 - 1975
Golden Landry	1974 - 1978
Babara Picard	1975 - 1982
Edward Hebert	1974 - 1982
Paul E. Catalon	1974 - 2005
Nason A. Trahan	1978 - 1998
Wayne Theriot	1982 - 1998
Marlene Theriot	1998 - 2002

145

Henry P. Trahan	1998 - 2002
Lee Wood	2002 - 2003
Troy Catalon	2005 - 2011
Darin J. DesOrmeaux	2003 -
Gary J. Villien	2003 -
Phyllis Catalon Johnson	2011 -

PLUMBING INSPECTOR

Henri Fred Broussard	1954-1967

OFFICIAL JOURNAL

Abbeville Meridional

EARLY ELECTION COMMISSIONERS

Alex Dupre Broussard	1926
Ulysse S. Broussard	1926

PLANNING COMMISSION

J.C. Meaux	1979
Carroll Comeaux	1979
Ollie J. Chargois	1979
Robert Delhommer	1979
Elodie H. Broussard	1979
Geraldine Chargois	1979
Ethel St. Julian	1979
James Broussard	1999
Geraldine Chargois	1999
Mickey Comboy	1999
Wayne Theriot	1999
Florence Trahan	1999
Marc J. Villien, M.D.	1999

POSTMASTERS

Maurice Villien
J.A. Villien, M.D.
Cyprien D. Trahan
Robert "Bob" L. Trahan
Jessie Champagne
Dale Dooley
Calvin R. Arrington, Jr.
Paul Thibodeaux

PROCLAMATIONS

1967
Firefighters Week   *October 15 – 21*
1968
Firefighters Day   *November 3*
1969
Maurice High School Basketball Week   *March 2 – 8*
Maurice Bulldog – Johnny Picard Day   *March 5*
Fire Prevention Week   *October 5 - 11*
1974
Municipal Clerk's Week   May 12 – 18
1986
Small Business Week   *May 18 – 24*
1988
Drug Free Week   *November 2 - 6*
1997
Rachel Martin Villien Day   *August 30*

Origin of Name. Jean-Maurice Villien was the architect and planner of the street layout in Maurice. His mercantile was the first commercial enterprise here, and his contributions toward building a school and church, together became known as Mauriceville. When the United States Postal Department established a post office within his store, *Le Magasin à Maurice,* the name for the post mark was designated as **Maurice**. A proclamation by residents of the community in 1911 declared the official name of the town as the **Village of Maurice**.

Date of Incorporation. The Village of Maurice was incorporated on **December 27, 1911**.

Area and Shape of Maurice. The Village of Maurice is basically rectangular in shape and approximately two square miles. The incorporated area in 1990 U.S. Census was one and seven-tenths square miles. Population density consisted of two hundred fifty-four persons per square mile and housing density was one hundred fourteen houses per square mile.

Schools. Presently, there is one public school in Maurice, **Cecil Picard Elementary School**. It consists of kindergarten through sixth grade. There is one private school, **A+ and A+ Too Daycare & Learning Center**. Maurice High School was moved from Maurice to a location two miles south of town, merged with Meaux High School and became North Vermilion High School.

MAURICE POPULATION AND HOUSING

Year	Population	Housing
1895	50	-
1911*	-	-
1920	328	-
1930	330	-
1940	420	-
1950	335	-
1960	411	-
1970	476	140
1980	478	176
1990	432	194
2000	642	276
2010	964	

* Not Included in 1910 U.S. Census

GENERAL DEMOGRAPHICS OF 2000

Population		642	
Race			
	White	508	79.1 percent
	Black	126	19.6 percent
	Other	8	1.3 percent
Sex			
	Male	325	50.6 percent
	Female	317	49.4 percent
Housing Units		276	

WARD FOUR (BROUSSARD COVE) POPULATION
(Minor Civil Divisions)

Year	Population
1895	1,000
1900	2,025
1910	2,566
1920	2,805
1930	2,875
1940	2,468
1950	1,833
1960	1,869
1970	2,175
1980	2,676
1990	-
2000	-

PASTORS OF ST. ALPHONSUS CATHOLIC CHURCH

l'Abbe Alphonse LeQuilleuc	1893
Fr. Ferdinand Grimaud	1893
Reverend Augustus Michel Rochard	1899
Father W. J. Heffernan	1908
Reverend Joseph Antoine Quenouillere	1908
Reverend Celestin Marius Chambon	1908
Reverend Desire Serrazin	1910
Reverend Louis Laroche	1910
Reverend Francis A. Buquet	1924
Father Francis Gerboud "Jabeaux"	1926
Father Pierre Marie Gruel	1927
Father Joseph Roman	1929
Father Clifford Gaudin	1945
Father Gommer Eugene Joseph Maurice Veekmans	1946
Reverend Louis Joseph Napoleon Bertrand	1954
Father Joseph Robert Dubuc	1967
Father Robert C. Landry	1974
Rev. Martin Leonards	1988
Father O. Joseph Breaux	2002

PASTORS OF ST. JOSEPH CATHOLIC CHURCH

Father Francis Wade	1946
Father Leander Martin	1954
Father Leo Weng	1955
Father Maurice Rousseve	1966
Father Charles Burns	1974
Father Konrad Wenzki	1974
Father Rodney Bowers	1984
Father Gus Wall	1984
Father Steven Schuler	1987
Brother James Fisher	1987
Father Charles Heskamp	1993
Father Willie Oliver	1996
Father Joseph Simon	1996
Father Richard Zawadzki	2003
Father Arockiam Arockiam	2005
Father Michael Sucharski	2010

CHRONOLOGY OF
MAURICE SCHOOL HISTORY

1877 Ward Four Schools were located on properties of Lazard Broussard and David Meaux

1878 Ward Four School was located on property of Jean Treville Broussard

1885 Ward Four School, Broussard Cove School, was located on property donated by Joseph Clark. Principals were, first Gerard Thibodeaux and then Alcibald Broussard.

1899 First School in Maurice (Maurice School) was located on property donated by Maurice Villien.

1899 Telesmar Delcambre was the first principal

1914 Principal, Rene T. Broussard

1914 Fire destroyed the school

1922 – 1923 Principal, Emile Ventre

1922 Maurice School was listed as a Junior High and Elementary School

1924 – 1925 Maurice School lost Junior High School funding.

1924 – 1926 Principal, I.R. Brumfield

1926 Maurice School built on Albert Street

1927 – 1930 Principal, U.Z. Baumgardner

1927 – 1928 Maurice School placed on the state Senior High School list.

1928 Maurice High School first Graduates (2)

1929 Maurice High won Parish Basketball Championship.

1934 Principal, O. L. Hebert

1934 – 1942 Principal, Leo L. Hebert

1937 Typewriting course first offered.

1939 Maurice High School Building dedicated by Vermilion Parish School Board (The dedication plaque was severely damaged in the 1981 fire and is on display at Cecil Picard Elementary.)

1942 Vermilion Parish basketball champions.

1942 – 1966 Principal, Romain Picard

1946 Maurice High graduated 24 Seniors.

1948 Maurice School first yearbook, *Bow Wow.*

1948 The last graduates completed eleven years of school

1948 Maurice High graduated 25 Seniors

1948 Yearbook dedicated to Anna Nugent Mouton

1949 Louisiana law required students to attend twelve years of school

1949 Maurice High graduated One (1) Senior (Henry Duhon)

1949 Yearbook dedicated to Rachel Martin Villien

1950 Maurice High graduated 12 Seniors

1950 Students that graduated received twelve years of education.

1950 Lunch Room and Canning Room

1950 W. Gayre Bazar was Music Director

1953 Band Building dedicated

1953 Maurice High graduated 12 Seniors

1953 Yearbook dedicated to Lona C. Broussard

1954 Maurice High won Louisiana State Track & Field Championship.

1955 Yearbook dedicated to Romain Picard

1956 Won state sweepstakes in Rally.

1957 Maurice High graduated 15 Seniors

1962 Ceiling fans installed in classrooms.

1963 First Secretary, Barbara Picard

1966 – 69 Principal, Cecil Picard

1966 Yearbook dedicated to Albert Villien Winch

1967 Yearbook dedicated to Roy F. Broussard

1969 Maurice High School won La. State "Class C" Track & Field Champs

1969 – 1980 Maurice High School Principal, Jules E. Duhon

1970 Maurice High graduated 25 seniors.

1970 Yearbook dedicated to Gabriel Dartez, Jr.

1971 Maurice High graduated 23 seniors

1973 Maurice High won Louisiana State Track & Field Championship. Class "B" School.

1973 Maurice High won Louisiana State Basketball Championship.

1973 First Boys and Girls baseball teams

1975 Maurice High won second place Louisiana State Baseball Championship.

1975 Yearbook dedicated to Dorothy Beaugh.

1976 Yearbook dedicated to Anna G. Rice.

1977 Maurice High won District 13-B Baseball Championship

1977 There were 49 graduates which was largest number to ever matriculate at one time.

1979 Maurice School student body: 579 students, 327 elementary and 252 high school.

1979 Yearbook dedicated to Lynn LeBlanc

1980 May, Maurice High School graduated their last senior class. The school completed the 1980 school year as Maurice High School (the last class to graduate) and close its doors as a high school.

1980 September, Maurice High School was moved to a new location four miles south of Maurice. Maurice High consolidated with Meaux, Leroy and Indian Bayou High Schools to form North Vermilion High School (grades 7–12).

1980 September, North Vermilion High School opened (7– 12 grade), Jules E. Duhon, Principal (he transferred from Maurice High School to North Vermilion).

1980 - 1988 Maurice Elementary School Principal, Cordell Dartez

1980 September, Maurice High School building converted to Maurice Elementary (grades K – 6).

1980 Final Maurice High School Yearbook dedicated to Jeffery DeRouen.

1981 February 11, Fire destroyed the Maurice Elementary School

1981 North Vermilion High School graduated their first High School Class

1986 Maurice Elementary School, new building constructed

1988 - 2005 Maurice Elementary School Principal, Patricia Webb

2005 Enrollment 490 students
2005-2008 Maurice Elementary School Principal, Greg Theriot
2007 Maurice Elementary School changed name to Cecil Picard Elementary
2007 – 2008 Cecil Picard Elementary School Principal, Greg Theriot
2008–2011 Cecil Picard Elementary School Principal, Wendy Stoute
2011 Enrollment at Cecil Picard Elementary School was approximately 700 students
2011-Present   Cecil Picard Elementary School Principal, Paulette Gaspard.

VERMION PARISH LIBRARY, MAURICE BRANCH
MAURICE LIBRARIANS

Edith Broussard	1944-64
Louise Broussard	1964-65
Marie P. Hebert	1965-68
Neddie Dartez	1968-89
Patricia W. Simon	1989-90
Judy Broussard	1990-93
Jackie Broussard	1993-94
Rita Allen	1994-94
Cheryl Bergeron	1994-

Figures

1   Early Years

1.1   Dr. J.A. Villien's residence, photo courtesy of Dr. Marc J. Villien.

1.2   Ward Map, Vermilion Parish Ward Map, courtesy of J.E. Shexnaider and Associates.

1.3   Brothers Joseph-Etienne and Jean-Maurice, photo courtesy of Villien Family collection.

1.4   1863 Plat Map of St. Mary Parish, courtesy of David C. Edmonds, *Yankee Autumn in Acadiana.*

1.5   Map of Milton, source: Robert P. Prejean, *The Story of Milton.*

1.6   1881 Homestead Map of Sections 1, 2, 11 and 12. Land Grants and Claims Map 1881, courtesy of Department of State of Louisiana Archives, Baton Rouge, Louisiana.

1.7   Aerial view of "The Grove," source: 1970 aerial by Douglas Villien.

1.8   Painting of The Grove and home of Jean-Maurice Villien by Douglas Villien, 2011.

1.9   Jean-Maurice Villien, photo courtesy of Villien Family collection.

1.10   Marie Chaty Villien, photo courtesy of Villien Family collection.

1.11   Plan of Maurice, First Plan of Maurice, Louisiana, Vermilion Parish Clerk of Court, Plat Book, Instrument #25714, pp.96. (note: map drawn by E. Montagne, Jr., ca. 1893, recorded in 1913).

1.12   Corine M. Broussard, courtesy of Francine Broussard Mathiew, Broussard Family collection.

1.13   La Chapelle à Maurice also known as L'Église de St. Alphonse, built in 1886, Villien family archives, courtesy of Paul O. Villien, Jr.

1.14   Le Magasin à Maurice, painting by Douglas L. Villien, Sr.

1.15   Le Magasin à Maurice on Church Street in 2009, photographer unknown.

1.16   Dr. Joseph A. Villien, photo courtesy of Villien Family collection.

1.17   Jean-Maurice Villien, Jr., photo courtesy of Jackie L. Truitt.

1.18   Villien Brothers and Company, photographer unknown.

1.19   Villien Brothers and Le Magasin à Maurice, photo courtesy of Dr. Paul O. Villien, Jr.

1.20   Villien Brothers, photo courtesy of Dr. Paul O. Villien, Jr.

1.21   Camille Jean Francois Broussard, courtesy of Johnette Broussard.

1.22   Aurelia Amelia Broussard, courtesy of Johnette Broussard.

1.23   Gifts from Jacques-Marie Villien to Dr. J.A. Villien, photos by Douglas L. Villien, Sr.

2   Beginnings of Business

2.1   Early Commerce, photo of Tom and Esther Baudoin gathering crops and Placide Broussard house in background, courtesy of Judy Dartez Lalande.

2.2   Albert Benedict Broussard, photo courtesy of Jackie LeBlanc Truitt.

2.3   Albert Camille Broussard, courtesy of Francine Broussard Mathiew, Broussard Family collection.

2.4   Broussard–Picard General Merchandise Store, ca. 1900, photo courtesy of Dr. David G. Trahan.

2.5   Jean Camille Broussard, courtesy of Suzanne Dartez Reed.

2.6   Hilaire Broussard, courtesy of Johnette Broussard.

3   Public Service

4   Post Office

5   Fire Department

6   Mid-Century Trade

7   A Village Foundation

8   A Place Called School

8.1   Maurice School, photo courtesy of Francine Broussard Mathiew.
8.2   Maurice School, ca. 1913 and Annette M. Gaidry, photo courtesy of Villien Family collection.
8.3   Maurice School, ca. 1914, photo courtesy of Villien Family collection.
8.4   Map of School site, from 1921 Sanborn Map, courtesy of Louisiana State Department of Archives.
8.5   1928 Maurice High School student body, photo courtesy of Loubert G. Trahan.
8.6   1928 Girls Basketball team, photo courtesy of Loubert G. Trahan.
8.7   1929 Boys Basketball team, photo courtesy of Loubert G. Trahan.
8.8   Maurice High School students, 1930s, photo courtesy of Johnette Broussard.
8.9   Maurice High School damaged by storm and flood, photos courtesy of Alberta Villien Winch.
8.10   Maurice High School class of 1946, photo courtesy of Alberta Villien Winch.
8.11   Elementary School Building, photo from 1948 *Bow Wow*, Maurice High School yearbook.
8.12   High School Building, photo from 1948 *Bow Wow*, Maurice High School yearbook.
8.13   1932 School Picnic, photo courtesy of the *Abbeville Meridional*.
8.14   Maurice High School and Romain Picard home was damaged, photos courtesy of Alberta Villien Winch.
8.15   First "Bow Wow" yearbook, photo courtesy of Douglas Villien.
8.16   Rachel Villien, First Grade Teacher, 1948 *Bow Wow*, from M.H.S. yearbook.
8.17   Alberta Villien, English Teacher, 1950 *Bow Wow*, from M.H.S. yearbook.
8.18   Louise Villien, Science Teacher, 1950 *Bow Wow*, from M.H.S. yearbook.
8.19   Band Building, photo courtesy of Douglas Villien.
8.20   Maurice Junior Band, from 1950 *Bow Wow*, Maurice High School yearbook.
8.21   Maurice High School Band, from 1954-55 *Bow Wow*, Maurice High School Yearbook.
8.22   1955 Athletic Court, from 1954-55 *Bow Wow*, Maurice High School yearbook.
8.23   Maurice High School Band, from 1968 *Bow Wow*, Maurice High School yearbook.
8.24   1973 High School Basketball State Champions, from 1973 *Bow Wow*, Maurice High School yearbook.
8.25   1973 High School Track and Field Class "C" State Champions, from 1973 *Bow Wow*, Maurice High School yearbook.
8.26   First Boys Baseball Team, from 1980 *Bow Wow*, Maurice High School yearbook.
8.27   First Girls Baseball Team, from 1980 *Bow Wow*, Maurice High School yearbook.
8.28   The Last *Bow Wow* yearbook cover, from 1980 *Bow Wow*, Maurice High School.
8.29   Maurice Elementary destroyed by fire in 1981, photo by Peter Piazza.
8.30   Romain Picard, Principal, from 1955 *Bow Wow* yearbook, Maurice High School.
8.31   Cecil J. Picard, Principal, from 1967 *Bow Wow* yearbook, Maurice High School.

9   Businesses of Today

10   A Plan for Tomorrow

Biographical

B.1   Mont Blanc, photo courtesy of Paul O. Villien, Jr., M.D.

B.2   Jean-Maurice Villien, photo courtesy of Villien Family collection.

B.3   Joseph-Etienne and Jean-Maurice, ca. 1855, photo courtesy of Villien Family collection.

B.4   Prairie Vermilion today, photo by Douglas Villien.

B.5   Jean-Maurice Villien, memorial card, courtesy of Dr. Paul O. Villien, Jr.; and A La Memoire de Maurice Villien, courtesy of Natasha Villien Legé.

B.6   Home of Dr. J.A. Villien, Sr., photo courtesy of Dr. Marc J. Villien.

B.7   Dr. J.A. Villien, Sr., photo courtesy of Villien Family collection.

B.8   Corine Marie Broussard, photo courtesy of Johnette Broussard, Broussard Family collection.

B.9   Hilaire D. Broussard, photo courtesy of Johnette Broussard, Broussard Family collection.

B.10   Jean Camille Broussard, photo courtesy of Suzanne Dartez Reed.

B.11   Ernest G. Trahan remembrance, photo courtesy of David G. Trahan.

B.12   Dr. Carroll J. Mouton, photo courtesy of the Village of Maurice.

B.13   Romain Picard, photo from *Bow Wow* yearbook, Maurice High School.

B.14   Cecil J. Picard, photo courtesy of Cecil Picard Elementary School.

B.15   Corbette A. LeBlanc, photo courtesy of the Village of Maurice.

B.16   Dr. Paul O. Villien, Sr., photo courtesy of Douglas Villien.

B.17   Rachel Martin Villien, photo from *Bow Wow* yearbook, Maurice High School.

B.18   Cyprien D. Trahan, photograph courtesy of David G. Trahan.

B.19   James Cyr Villien, photo courtesy of Thom Wynne.

B.20   Alberta Octavia Villien Winch, photo from *Bow Wow* yearbook, Maurice High School.

B.21   Chief H. Fred Broussard, photo courtesy of Maurice Volunteer Fire Department.

B.22   Albert Armel Villien, photo courtesy of Villien Family collection.

B.23   Barbara L. Picard, photo courtesy of the Village of Maurice.

B.24   Robert H. Ferguson, photo courtesy of the Village of Maurice.

B.25   Wayne Theriot, photo courtesy of the Village of Maurice.

B.26   Alexander Bruce Mouton, photo courtesy of Lynn Mouton Spence.

Bibliography

BOOKS

Bow Wow. Taylor Publishing Company, Dallas, TX, 1948, 1949. Maurice High School Yearbooks from private collection of Edgar Baudoin, November 2010.

Bow Wow. Taylor Publishing Company, Dallas, TX, 1950, 1959, 1957. Maurice High School Yearbooks from private collection of Elgin Prejean Baudoin, November, 2010.

Bow Wow. Taylor Publishing Company, Dallas, TX., 1966, 1967, 1968, 1969, 1970, 1971, 1973, 1974, 1975, 1976, 1977. Maurice High School Yearbooks from private collection of Elizabeth Baudoin Landry, November, 2010.

Bow Wow. Taylor Publishing Company, Dallas, TX., 1953, 1978, 1979, 1980. Maurice High School Yearbooks from Library of North Vermilion High School, November, 2010.

Davis, Edwin Adams. *Louisiana The Pelican State*. Louisiana State University Press, Baton Rouge, Louisiana, 1976.

Edmonds, David C. *Yankee Autumn in Acadiana: A narrative of the great Texas overland expedition through southwestern Louisiana, October-December, 1863*. The Acadiana Press, Lafayette, Louisiana, 1979, (Confederate Map of St. Mary Parish/National Archives).

Fortier, Alcée, Lit. D., ed. *Louisiana, Comprising sketches of parishes, towns, events, institutions, and persons, arranged in cyclopedic form*, Vol. I, Louisiana, Century Historical Association, 1914.

Germann, John J., w/ Alan H. Patera and John S. Gallagher. *Louisiana Post Offices*. The Depot, Lake Grove, Oregon, 1990.

Jr. Patriots, Maurice Elementary School Yearbook, Taylor Publishing Company, Dallas, TX., 1985.

Maurice Elementary, Yearbook, Taylor Publishing Company, 1980.

Patriots, Cecil Picard Elementary School Yearbook, Taylor Publishing Company, 1981.

Perrin, William Henry, ed. *Southwest Louisiana Biographical and Historical*, 2 parts, New Orleans, The Gulf Publishing Company, 2 parts, 1891.

Post, Lauren C., *Cajun Sketches,* Louisiana State University Press, Baton Rouge, LA, 1974.

Trillin, Calvin. *70555 Turducken Town*. National Geographic Magazine, November 2005.

United States Official Postal Guide, Vol. I, July 1939: Louisiana, Vermilion Parish, Maurice, P.O. No. 45885, Unit 2588. (Washington, D.C., United States Government Printing Office, 1939).

Vermilion Historical Society. *History of Vermilion Parish Louisiana, Vol. 1,* Taylor Publishing Company, Dallas, TX, 1983.

Vermilion Historical Society. *History of Vermilion Parish Louisiana, Vol. 2,* Taylor Publishing Company, Dallas, TX, 2003.

Villien, Jr., Paul O., M.D. *Villien-Chaty Family, Vol.1*. [self]. New Orleans, Louisiana, January, 2009.

Villien, Jr., Paul O., M.D.. *Villien-Chaty Family, Vol.2*. [self]. New Orleans, Louisiana, 2010.

PUBLIC RECORDS, REPORTS AND ARCHIVES

Book of Minutes, *Village of Maurice Public Records, 1911 – 2011*, Maurice, Louisiana, City Hall.

Community Design Workshop: Maurice, Louisiana.(University of Louisiana at Lafayette, School of Architecture and Design, 2010)

Plan of Maurice, Louisiana, Vermilion Parish Clerk of Court, Plat Book, Instrument #25714, pp.96. (note: map drawn ca. 1893, recorded in 1913).

Washington D.C., Library of Congress. *French and American Claims Commission, No. 171.* J. M. Villien vs. The United States, February 21, 1881.

Louisiana, Department of State, Sanborn Map Company. *Fire Prevention Map 1921, Maurice, Louisiana.* (New York, New York, 1921). Photo courtesy of Vermilion Historical Society, November 23, 2010.

Louisiana State Land and Natural Resources, Historical Records. *U.S. Tract Book. Vol. 8.*
Louisiana, General Land Office Map, South Western District. December 24, 1881.

Taylor, Gertrude C., Carl A. Brasseaux, and Glenn R. Conrad, compiled by. *Land Grants, Land Claims, and Land Sales, 1821 – 1856*: of the lower Vermilion River Area. Louisiana, Attakapas Historical Association, 1983.

Vermilion Parish, Conveyance Records, Office of Clerk of Court. *Conveyance Book No. 6416.* (Corine M. Broussard to Maurice Villien, April 9, 1894).

Vermilion Parish Resources and Facilities: Survey by Vermilion Parish Development Board. (State of Louisiana, Department of Public Works Planning Division, 1964).

ONLINE

Breaux, Reverend O., Joseph, Pastor. *St. Alphonsus Catholic Church.* Maurice, Louisiana, http://www.stalphonsus-maurice.org, (accessed September 2010).

Ludlow, Maxfield, Deputy Surveyor of Southwestern District. *Field Notes of Territory of New Orleans.* Louisiana: State Land Office, 1809.
http://wwwslodms.doa.la.gov/WebForms/Default.aspx?docId=507.00640&category= H#90, (accessed January 16, 2011).

National Fallen Firefighters Foundation, Maryland, Emmitsburg, http://dev.firehero.org/firehero/firefighter/query (accessed December 2011).

Sucharski, Reverend Mike, SVD. *St. Joseph Catholic Church,* http://www.stjoseph-maurice.org/4.html. (accessed December 2010).

United States Census 1920, *State Compendium Louisiana,* http://www2.census.gov/prod2/decennial/documents/0622968v14-19ch4.pdf. (accessed February 2011).

United States Census Bureau, United States Census 2000, http://www.census.gov/census2000/states/us.html. (accessed January 2011).

U.S. Census Bureau, http://search.census.gov/search?q=village+defined

Villien 1893, Himandus.net, (Daily Advertiser, 1893) http://www.himandus.net/hofh/chauvin/villien/villien_01_maurice_1831-1902.html , (accessed October 2010).

ARTICLES

Abbeville Meridional. Another Historical Note. (Abbeville Meridional, September 13, 1981).

Abbeville Meridional. Quota system bad for Maurice, Comment, (Abbeville Meridional, June 18, 1982).

Abbeville Meridional, Editorial: looking back, February 11, 1994.

Bradshaw, Jim, *Maurice Bank Robbery Was Bloody* Affair, Eunice, Louisiana, *The Eunice News,* April 11, 2010. Vol. 107, No. 29.

Daily Advertiser. *Dr. Villien, 88, Retired area banker_dies,* (Lafayette, Louisiana, *Daily Advertiser,* November 5, 1958).

Harrington, Pat. *Maurice Park Finish, dedicated. Abbeville Meridional,* June 29, 1983.

Kays, Tracy. *Retiring mayor holds memories of his village, Abbeville Meridional,* April 11, 1982. (courtesy of Jackie L. Truitt, January 2011).

Konczal, Michael. *Maurice's small town atmosphere is just fine with Barbara Picard,* (date unknown), *Lafayette, Daily Advertiser.*

Lindlof, Christine. *Recent Years Progressive Ones For Maurice Village,* Lafayette, Louisiana, *Daily Advertiser,* 1971.

Robichaux, Mark. *For holiday diners fickle about fowl there's turducken: An old Cajun connection Frankenstein would love flies off grocery shelves.* Massachusetts, Eastern Edition, Wall Street Journal, November 27, 1996.

Rosa, Chris. *Maurice getting apartment complex. Abbeville Meridional,* http://vermiliontoday.com/view/full_story/8159968/article-Maurice-getting-72-apartment-complex? (accessed March 6, 2011).

Times Picayune. Dr. J.A. Villien, Maurice, Dies. (New Orleans, Louisiana, November 6, 1958).
Tiny Maurice's Unopposed Mayor Chalks Big Plans For Its Future. (Daily Advertiser, Lafayette, Louisiana, ca. 1962).
Villiens Typify Early Spirit, Another Historical Note. Abbeville Meridional, September 13, 1981, 3.

NEWSPAPERS

Abbeville Meridional, Abbeville, Louisiana
The Daily Advertiser, Lafayette, Louisiana
Morning Advocate, Baton Rouge, Louisiana
The Advocate, Baton Rouge, Louisiana
The Eunice News, Eunice, Louisiana
The Times Picayune, New Orleans, Louisiana

PRIVATE ARCHIVES AND UNPUBLISHED WORKS

Caldwell, Alex, correspondence, March 19 and April 11, 2011.
Comeaux, Carroll, Rod Broussard & Matthew Trahan. *Maurice Volunteer Fire Department.* (Maurice Fire Department, January 21, 2010).
Prejean, Robert P. *The Story of Milton,* (no date or publisher) bound copy of file Vermilion Parish Library, Maurice, Louisiana.
Trahan, David G., Family photo collection, February 2011.
Villien Family oral history, papers and archives.
Villien, Sr., Paul O., DDS, miscellaneous notes and oral history.
Villien, Sr., Paul O., DDS. *Memoirs of Paul O. Villien,* 1961.

FEDERAL CENSUS REPORTS

U.S. Census of Population of the United States, 1880, 1890, 1900, 1910 – The Parish of Vermilion, Louisiana, Minor Civil Divisions 1910, 1900, 1890, 1880, Table 1, National Archives, Washington, D.C.
U.S. Eighth Census of Population, 1860: Louisiana, Parish of St. Martin, County of Attakapas, New Iberia Post Office. Washington, D.C., National Archives. 127
U.S. Ninth Census of Population, 1870: Louisiana, Parish of Vermilion, Abbeville Post Office. Washington, D.C., National Archives. roll 534, 203.
U.S. Eleventh Census of Population, 1890: Louisiana, Parish of Vermilion. Washington, D.C., National Archives.
U.S. Twelfth Census of Population, 1900: Louisiana, Parish of Vermilion. Washington, D.C., National Archives, June 1, 1900.
U.S. Thirteenth Census of Population, 1910: Louisiana, Parish of Vermilion. Washington, D.C., National Archives, April 15, 1910.
U.S. Fourteenth Census of Population, 1920: Louisiana, Parish of Vermilion, Maurice. Washington, D.C., National Archives, April 10, 1920.
U.S. Fourteenth Census of Population, 1921: *State Compendium Louisiana, Population of Parishes by Minor Civil Divisions, Table 2,* Bureau of the Census Library, Washington, D.C., April 14, 1921.
U.S. Fifteenth Census of Population, 1930. Louisiana, Parish of Vermilion, Maurice. National Archives, Washington, D.C., April 1, 1930.
U.S. Census of Population 2000, Washington, D.C., United States Census Bureau.
U.S. Census of Population2010.
http://www.census.gov/geo/www/2010census/.

INTERVIEWS, CORRESPONDENCE
AND ORAL HISTORY

Arrington, Calvin R., Jr., January 2011.
Broussard, Claude J., December 8, 2010.
Broussard, Doris C., January 18, 2011.
Broussard, Garrett, January 5, 2012.
Broussard, Johnette, June 25, 2012.
Broussard, Wallace, January 18, 2011.
Broussard, Willie A., January 18, 2011.
Baudoin, Gerard, December 8, 2010.
Baudoin, Edgar, October 11, 2010.
Bunnell, Martha V., September 2011.
Caldwell, Alexander, March 19, April 8, 2011.
Catalon, Doris, February 23, 2011.
Catalon, Joseph Emanuel, February 23, 2011.
Comboy, Sonia LeBlanc, November 3, 2010.
Comeaux, Carroll, January 18, 2011.
Dartez, Gerald, January 6, 2012.
Dartez, Cordell, January 5, 2011, March 24, 2011.
Dupuis, Mary Beth Trahan, April 13, 2011.
Edmonds, David C., April 6, 2011.
Ferguson, Robert "Bob", April 2010.
Gaspard, Paulette, June 24, 2011.
Hebert, Edvard, April 26, 2011.
Hebert, Joe, April 11, 2011.
Hebert, Ken "Keno," April 13, 2011.
House, Barbara, March 8, 2011.
Leger, Natasha Villien, May 31, 2011.
Miller, James "Jimbo", April 25, 2011.
Miller, Joe, April 24, 2011.
Picard, Barbara, December 8, 2010.
Reed, Suzanne Dartez, May 19, 2012.
Reed, Terrell K., January 2011.
Rost, Warren H., December 8, 2010.
Spence, Lynn Mouton, May 15, 2012
Stoute, Wendy, November 3, 2010, April 21, 2011.
Theriot, Wayne, January – April 2011.
Theriot, Greg, April 20, 2011.
Trahan, Loubert G, January 18, 2011, January 23, 2011, February 1, 18, 2011, November 23,
          2011, March 22, 2012, June 5, 2012.
Trahan, David G., D.D.S., February 23, 2011.
Trahan, Matthew, January 18, 2011.
Truitt, Jacqueline LeBlanc, August 16, 2011.
Villien, Cathy Broussard, April 12, 2011.
Villien, Fred O., Jr., January 16, 2011.
Villien, George C. Jr., "Buzzy," February 16, 2011.
Villien, Jr., Paul O., oral history, 2009 -2012.
Villien, Sr., Paul O., Family oral history, as related to him by Dr. J.A. Villien.
Villien, Sr., Paul O., Personal notes and interview with Maude G. Villien, July 12, 1991.
Villien, Sr., Paul O., Miscellaneous personal notes and oral history as related by Paul O. Villien, Sr.
Villien, Stephanie, September 15, 2010.
Vincent, Lynwood, April 26, 2011.
Webb, Patricia, April 21, 2011.
Winch, Alberta Villien, September 15, 2010; January 18, 2011; March 20, 2011; April 27, 2011;
          May 31, 2011, March 16, 2012, April 10, 2012, May 15, 2012, May 29, 2012, June 5,
          2012.

164

Index

171

173

176

W

X – Y - Z

Douglas L. Villien, Sr. is a freelance writer and land planning consultant in Baton Rouge, Louisiana. He has published articles about Maurice, Louisiana, its settlers and its history in *Vermilion Today* and the *Abbeville Meridional*. He is the great-grandson of the founder of Maurice and lives in Baton Rouge, Louisiana, with his wife.

Back Cover
The award winning photo was taken in April 1997 by Dr. Richard P. Villien of Lafayette, Louisiana. This photograph was the home of prominent Vermilion Parish physician, businessman and planter, Dr. J.A. Villien, Sr. The photo also includes a rare glimpse of Comet Hale-Bopp, seen in the western sky above the residence.

The home is a visual centerpiece in the Village of Maurice, Louisiana, and presently the residence of Dr. Marc J. Villien. Brothers, Dr. Richard P. Villien and Dr. Marc J. Villien are great-grandsons of the town's founder, Jean-Maurice Villien. The home was built in 1895 and is listed on the National Register of Historic Places.

Made in the USA
Monee, IL
21 January 2021

58257810R00115